CAMPBELL AUG 20 '82

PIECES OF THE PAST
A Story of Gilroy

Revised Edition

In celebration of Gilroy!
Claudia Salewske

Researched and Written
by
Claudia Kendall Salewske

367448
Copyright May 1982

SANTA CLARA COUNTY LIBRARY
SAN JOSE, CALIFORNIA

SANTA CLARA COUNTY LIBRARY
• 3 3305 00077 5456

Additional copies and mail order information available by writing to:
Pieces of the Past
P.O. Box 2241
Gilroy, California 95020

Typography and Layout: Gloria Appleby
Gloria's Graphics
Morgan Hill, California

Photo Preparation and Printing: Larry Kwong
The Printing Spot
Gilroy, California

Book Binding: Thomas G. Schenkel
Quality Trade Bindery
Santa Clara, California

Copyright © May, 1982

Acknowledgments

This book would not have been possible without the gracious cooperation of many people. I would like to acknowledge their contributions here.

I would first of all like to thank my friend Susan Pate who set my feet on the path of Gilroy's history. Next, to Joyce Flanigan and the Gilroy Unified School District who gave me the opportunity to write the children's history of our city, and encouraged this revision, my heartfelt thanks.

I am deeply grateful to Mary Prien, Director of the Gilroy Historical Museum, for her tireless efforts to aid my research, and her never-ending cheerful support. Her assistant, Patricia Snar Simon was of great help with the artwork for this text.

In addition the following people gave generously of their time and knowledge to aid this project:

George Willson White, Howard F. Smith, James C. Williams, Jack Martin, Leland Sanders, Clyde Arbuckle, F. Ralph Rambo, Mineko Sakai, William Sandoe Hanna, Stuart Fletcher, John Roffinella, Gail Bridwell, Ralph Johnson, Roy Lindeleaf, Harry P. Learnard, Dr. Rudy Melone, Forrest Barriger, Byron Bolfing.

The Gilroy Historical Society

The Gilroy Historical Museum — All photographs in this book unless otherwise credited, appear courtesy of the Museum.

And last, but certainly not least, to my entire family, especially my husband and our children, my appreciation for your loving support and faith which kept me going.

Claudia Kendall Salewske

Table of Contents

The Costanoan Indians..1
The Arrival of the Spanish..4
John Cameron Gilroy Arrives in the Rancho Era.........................7
Other Settlers...10
More of Our Valley is Settled..15
Henry Miller...17
Other Firsts...21
Early Schools and Growth of Our District.............................24
The First Churches...29
Subdivisions in Pleasant Valley?.....................................31
Timber!..31
Pleasant Valley Becomes the City of Gilroy...........................34
Hotels in Gilroy...35
The Redwood Retreat..39
Our Early Firefighters...41
The Music Hall . . . The Opera House.................................42
The Agricultural Industry . . . Neighbors from Other Lands...........45
    From France..45
    Seeds..47
    From Japan...47
    Europeans and the Dairy Industry.................................49
The Gilroy Brewery . . . Gilroy's Tobacco Industry...................51
Southern Europeans . . . Wineries and the Canning Industry...........52
The Garlic Capital...55
The Grange...57
The Chinese..57
The Newspapers of Gilroy...59
Healthcare for Gilroy..61
Some of Those Who Gave Generously to Gilroy..........................62
    Linwood Wheeler..62
    Caroline Amelia Hoxett...63
More About Some Historic Public Buildings............................64
The Chamber of Commerce..67
Other Names Gilroyans Remember.......................................67
The Strand Theatre...68
The Mill Road Park...70
The Gymkhana...72
The End of Our Story...74

17½" x 22½" copies of this map are available at the Gilroy Museum.

1. S.P.R.R. DEPOT.
2. R.R. HOUSE.
3. SOUTHERN PACIFIC HOTEL.
4. GILROY FLOURING MILL.
5. WHITEHURST & HODGES PLANING MILL.
6. EUREKA HOSE COS BUILDING.
7. ODD FELLOWS BUILDING.
8. WILLIAMS HOUSE.
9. SEVERANCE SEMINARY.
10. EPISCOPAL CHURCH.
11. MUSIC HALL.
12. VIGILANT ENGINE COS BUILDING.
13. PRESBYTERIAN CHURCH.
14. M.E. CHURCH.
15. MASONIC BUILDING.
16. M.E. CHURCH SOUTH.
17. PUBLIC SCHOOL BUILDING.
18. CHRISTIAN CHURCH.
19. ST. MARYS CATHOLIC CHURCH AND CONVENT OF THE IMMACULATE HEART.

F.W. BLAKE, PUB, GILROY, CAL.

Introduction

"The end of all our explorations will be to come back to where we began and discover the place for the first time." —T.S. Eliot

Our Garlic Festival, and our claim to be "The Garlic Capital of the World" have made Gilroy quite a celebrity city in recent years.

The recognition gained by our Festival is certainly a fine thing. But Gilroy, known as Pleasant Valley in the early days, had much to be proud of long before the first garlic was planted here.

In this book, I have attempted to take you on a journey through our city's past. This is by no means a complete history of Gilroy. But whether you are a long-time Gilroyan, and can reminisce as you read it . . . or a newcomer with no knowledge of the city's background, I hope this book will spark your desire to learn more.

Once you have travelled from the tranquil existence of our Coast Indians, through the lively Rancho days, the post 49er expansion, and finally into the Gilroy of this bustling twentieth century, I hope that you will see our city in a new light. Many of the places you will read about are gone now. However, a good number of them remain for you to experience. Furthermore, I hope that you will take part in the historic walking tours offered by the Theatre Angels Art League and our Gilroy Historical Society. Hopefully, you'll be inspired to take walks on your own as well!

As you journey along these pathways of the past, may they bring you to a better understanding of this city called Gilroy. And for those to whom Gilroy is home, may they also leave you with a strong sense of your place in our city's future.

Claudia Kendall Salewske
Gilroy, California
May 1982

The Costanoan Indians

The origin of the Costanoans (or Coast Dwellers) is not easily traced. Anthropologists feel that their facial conformation and similarities in habits suggest ties with the tribes of the Aleutian Islands, and possibly with the primitive peoples of Asia and the Orient. This would support the "land bridge" migration theory. Their villages stretched from the northern shores of San Francisco Bay down through the Salinas Valley.

Courtesy Ralph Rambo

The Costanoans are a subgroup of the large Penutian family of tribes which covered many parts of California at one time. Each of the tribes within this "family" had a very distinct dialect. The language could even differ from village to village within the same tribe. In our valley, however, the several dialects amongst the Costanoans appear to have been closely related and were called "Mut-San".

Research on the Costanoan culture is confounded by the fact that these natives had no written language. As a result, our limited knowledge of them comes mostly from the observations of others. Often the information is conflicting.

For example, there are references to these Indians recorded in the diary of the Spaniard Vizcaino, who came to our shores in 1602. He noted the heavy population of Costanoans, and remarked that they appeared to be a friendly, orderly people. Other Spaniards saw them less favorably and used terms like wild, dirty, and stupid to describe these early inhabitants.

The Costanoans lived a simple sort of life. Food was so abundant in this area that the Indians were not compelled to develop an agricultural system. They existed from day to day on what nature provided.

Their main diet was acorns, berries, mushrooms, pine nuts, and wild seeds and fruit. One "delicacy" was grasshoppers. The women and children would collect them in the fields. They were roasted in the coals of the cooking fire, and served as a munchy snack. These Indians also grubbed for caterpillar and beetle larvae as food sources, and even for roots. When the American pioneers began arriving here they looked upon these practices with contempt, and called them "Digger Indians".

Courtesy Ralph Rambo

The Costanoans also fished, mostly for what could be caught in nearby streams. However, large mounds of buried shells have been uncovered, particularly in the Uvas Canyon where a large village once existed. At times these people must have ventured over to the coastline and gathered in their nets the abalone, clams, mussels and other food sources that the seashore provides. In addition, their diet was supplemented with small game, caught in snares. And on occasion, deer and bear were brought down with a bow and arrow.

The baskets they used were woven from all available resources--tules, roots, reeds, grass and sticks. Hot pitch was applied to make the baskets water-tight. The women created these containers in several shapes and sizes to meet their various needs. One jug-like basket was a practical favorite. Often food for a meal was gathered, prepared and served all in this one basket.

Courtesy Ralph Rambo

I recommend to you the Museum at the New Almaden Mine, south of San Jose. Owner/Curator Constance Perham has a fine display there of articles of the Costanoan culture, in addition to many other exhibits. In studying a cradleboard fashioned by an Indian woman, I was struck by the ingenuity of these early mothers. Today's infant seats are no more clever.

The weaving skills of the Costanoans were put to use in constructing their homes as well. The circular wikiups, usually about six feet in diameter, were most often built of supple willow boughs, and covered with thatching and mud. A smoke hole was left at the top. Animal skins used for bedding were the only furnishings. These shelters were no match for the heavy winter rains. During those months the Indians moved into caves.

In the warm weather these natives wore little clothing. Again, this was something that incoming white man later saw as "savage". The women fashioned skirts out of tule grass and animal skins. The men wore a loincloth, if anything, usually made of deerskin. In the winter months both men and women donned cloaks of animal skins to ward off the cold.

The women observed a sensible practice of stringing necklaces made of pieces of abalone shells. This "jewelry" was worn particularly when they were gathering food. As they knelt down in the fields, the sun would reflect off the shells. This glaring light would disturb the rattlesnakes which were plentiful in this terrain. The rattling sound alerted the women, and they could retreat unharmed.

The Costanoans were a social people. Periodically the inhabitants of several villages would get together, and the partying would go on for several days. The women prepared a great deal of food, and the eating, singing, dancing and sporting games were enjoyed by all ages.

One favorite practice at these ceremonial times was that of body painting. The Indians would journey up to the deep caves below Loma Prieta Mountain near San Jose. The cinnabar ore found in these caves is a mixture

Oakland Art Museum

of mercury plus sulphur, and is deep red in color. The Costanoans called it "mohetka". They would pulverize the ore, then mix it with animal fat to form a body makeup. This would be applied to their entire being as the picture here indicates. Patterns were made, alternating with a whitish-grey paste, probably made from ashes or ground rock. Berry juice and the stain from nuts provided other colors.

Many an Indian became quite ill from the application of cinnabar "paint". This ore, with its high concentration of mercuric sulphide was absorbed through the pores, causing excessive salivation and sores in the mouth and gums. Occasionally, perhaps due to dehydration and/or infection, this blood poisoning proved fatal. When the educated mission padres settled here, they were able to deduce that the illness which which mystified the natives was chemically induced. They rapidly saw to it that the Indians discontinued this harmful custom.

We have little information about the religious beliefs of these early people. As mentioned before, theirs was a simple, peaceful existence. They apparently revered all of nature, and felt that the redwood groves held sacred spirits. It is thought that they didn't worship one supreme being, but rather continuously sought to appease the "evil spirits" they believed were afoot in their world.

In summation, the Costanoans were called "children of nature" by the mission fathers. Perhaps it was this childlike quality which led to their eventual massive annihilation. They were no match for the wily, ambitious white men, whose infiltration of their lands became more and more of a hostile domination. And while it is true that theirs was not a profound and lasting

Courtesy Ralph Rambo

impact upon our valley's past, their place in our history was nonetheless an important one. We must remember that it was due to the Indian's mere presence here that cause existed to establish our mission system. The physical labors of the Costanoans, as with other tribes in their respective territories, contributed to the creation of the picturesque mission landmarks which form a chain along our Pacific coastline. Perhaps we might consider these structures, at least in part, as the Indian's legacy to their land which was destined to become the state of California.

The Arrival of the Spanish

To see the colorful Spanish era in its proper framework, we need to go back in time. In 1521, a viceroyalty called New Spain was formed, which generally encompassed the territory now known as the southwest portion of the United States, Mexico, Central America north of Panama, the West Indies, and even the Phillippines. Mexico City was the seat of this government. It was from this point that many of the Spanish-speaking settlers to our area arrived. We noted previously that many explorers returned home with accounts of the "rancherias" or villages of uncivilized natives. This news, combined with the reports of superb geographical conditions to the north, made Alta California the logical direction in which to expand Spanish land holdings.

In 1768, in response to an order from the King of Spain to secure California before the Russians moving in from the North could do the same, a group of Franciscan friars under the direction of Father Junipero Serra left lower California. Their intent was to peacefully convert Upper or Alta California. The initial link in the mission chain which would eventually spread six-hundred miles up the coast was formed by these padres on July 16, 1769, as Mission San Diego.

Also in this same year, Gaspar de Portola was sent with a party by order of the Visitador (Inspector) General to New Spain to take charge of and fortify the ports of San Diego and Monterey. It is known that when their ship reached northern waters, it passed by Monterey Bay, probably because of heavy fog. The crew put in to shore near San Pedro instead.

From this point, Portola's scout, Jose Francisco de Ortega, explored further north, and is credited with having discovered the San Francisco Bay. Members of the party also climbed over the Coast Range and had their first look at our Santa Clara Valley. On a later overland expedition Monterey Bay was located. The first huts were built there in 1776.

Courtesy Ralph Rambo

Pedro Fages is thought to be the first white man to follow an inland route from Monterey Bay to San Francisco Bay. His initial trip was made in 1770. Two years later he made a second journey, which was recorded by Fray Juan Crespí. They departed from Monterey on March 20th of 1772, came over the Gabilan Mountains, and on March 22nd pitched camp on a stretch of Llagas Creek, just a little north of Gilroy. He, like the others before him, had peaceful encounters with the Costanoans.

The expedition of Juan Bautista DeAnza took place in 1775-76. Colonists in this party came overland from Sonora, Mexico, bringing with them livestock and supplies. Their destination was Monterey. This journey opened up a vital inland supply route.

The missionary fathers who accompanied nearly every exploration party as it ventured northward had one main task before them . . . the founding of sites where they could live among the Indian people and teach them not only Christianity, but the fundamentals of education such as reading, writing, and numbers.

Father Serra was director or presidente of the growing mission system of California. To oversee these institutions effectively, Father Serra felt it was imperative that the missions be within a day's walking distance of one another. Accordingly, in 1795, the padres sought and were granted permission from Mexico City to establish another mission between the San Carlos Borromeo de Carmel and the Santa Clara Missions. On June 24, 1797, the Mission San Juan Bautista, the fifteenth and largest in the chain was formally dedicated.

Large amounts of fertile land were a part of the grounds of each of the missions. Crops were raised as well as herds of livestock. Here the Indians were taught the agricultural skills they did not come by naturally. More clothing was insisted upon. The mission attire that was issued to the natives, as the photograph shows, reflected the European culture. As to their education, apparently our natives delighted in the music that was shared with them, and learned it easily. However, the padres labored to teach the Indians their three R's. There were some among their charges who were model students. However the majority of Indians were, after many an exasperating lesson, considered too dull of mind to learn anything but the very basics, like counting to twenty. I wonder if cultural differences entered in. It's possible that all of this "book learning" didn't seem relevant to our natives. Therefore grasping it came low on their list of priorities!

Many bewildered and unhappy Indians escaped from the missions and resumed a life in the wild. In 1826, the federal government forwarded a directive to the authorities in California that the Indians were to be liberated. Further word came from Mexico that the missions were never intended to be permanent establishments. Rather, they were a stepping stone toward the forming of Indian settlements which would function in a parish system.

The Indians carried tallow from the mission down to the ships harbored in Monterey Bay for trading.

This transfer of power from church to state brought ruination to the mission wealth that the fathers had built up over the years. The vast herds of valuable livestock were divided among administrators and their friends and family. The land was likewise often granted as a favor to a friend. The Indians, ignorant of how to stop this wave of take-over suffered most. In the ensuing years, the white men who were coming to the west in increasing numbers brought with them two kinds of trouble. Many who had experienced meetings with unfriendly tribes while crossing the plains, took no time to establish rapport. Confronted by an Indian, they assumed it was kill or be killed. Many Costanoans, and indeed Indians in all parts of California, were slaughtered this way. In addition, the white man brought his diseases for which the Indians had no resistance. Countless hundreds succumbed to plagues of thyphoid, cholera, smallpox, measles and the like. In all, the treatment of her natives by those intending to "civilize" California is a sad page in our state's history.

California and her missions were under the rule of Spanish governors from 1770-1822. Spanish rule was replaced by Mexican jurisdiction in 1822. Mexican rule continued until the sovereignty of the United States was established at the end of the Mexican War with the States in 1847.

The Mission at San Juan Bautista was established in 1797. John and Maria Clara Gilroy were married here in 1821.

Our community today is comprised of many citizens whose roots trace back to the early settlers who came here from Spain and New Spain. Many Hispanic traditions and celebrations are still observed here, adding to the rich cultural diversity that is a part of life in Gilroy.

John Cameron Gilroy Arrives in the Rancho Era

During the periods of Spanish and Mexican rule of California, the governors in charge divided the land into parcels called ranchos. In our area the ranchos ranged in size from about two hundred acres to forty thousand acres.

The rancho days were a vibrant era in California's history. Life pulsated to the rhythm of castanets and guitars. Cattle raising was the chief livelihood. Every rancho could boast of many fine equestrians, most of whom were also adept with a lariat. Many of the inhabitants were a mixture of native Indian and Castilian Spanish. They were a handsome and vigorous race.

Hospitality was one of their chief virtues. Travellers along the mission route, the El Camino Real as it was known, were warmly welcomed. Fiestas were a common occurrence, and dancing the fandango and playing cards were favorite amusements.

The village of San Ysidro was just such a place. It was into this lively Rancho setting that John Cameron Gilroy wandered in the year 1814.

He was born in 1794 in Inverness-shire, which is in the far north of Scotland. As a young teenager he left home to go to sea. There are some reports that just prior to this, his family moved to England. It is thought that perhaps at this time he changed his last name from Cameron to Gilroy, Gilroy being his mother's maiden name.

Young John was a seaman aboard the *Issac Todd*, a vessel belonging to the Hudson Bay Company, when it arrived in Monterey harbor in February of 1814. Some histories state that he was put ashore sick with scurvy. Another story is that he fled the ship, having struck one of its officers during an argument. Fearing severe reprisal, so this version goes, he and a shipmate known as Deaf Jimmy set off in search of a less troublesome environment. By this account, it was in these circumstances that he changed his last name to Gilroy to avoid detection.

These discrepancies aside, John Gilroy and Deaf Jimmy walked to Mission San Juan Bautista, and then moved on to the village of San Ysidro. His companion continued north, but Gilroy remained here, becoming the first non-Spanish settler in California.

Rancho San Ysidro was the home of Don Ygnacio Ortega and his wife Gertrudis Arce Ortega. The Rancho was one of the few Spanish land grants, given over to Ortega in 1810, according to Hubert Howe Bancroft. Don Ortega was the son of Jose Francisco Ortega, Portola's scout who was mentioned earlier.

Brand of Rancho San Ysidro

John Gilroy was a tall, handsome young man with an easy, pleasant manner. Although he was welcomed in his new location, with the language barrier and the cultural differences, he was apparently homesick for a time and even considered returning to the British Isles. This feeling passed, and it wasn't long before he learned the Spanish language and became an active member in the community.

In September of 1814 the young Scotsman was baptized Juan Bautista Maria Gilroy at the Carmel Mission. He was given permission by the Viceroy of Mexico City to remain in California and to marry.

Gilroy rented some land from Don Ortega and bought several cows. A diligent man, he soon was prospering. One of Don Ortega's daughters was the lovely Maria Clara de la Asuncion. In 1821, Maria Clara and John Gilroy were married at the Mission San Juan Bautista. Over the years, seventeen children were born to the couple, but only nine survived.

Don Ortega's home was one of those which was not far off the El Camino Real. Many a weary traveler stayed overnight at the spacious Rancho enjoying a hearty meal and the good company of the Ortega family.

When all the Ortega relations gathered together for a fiesta, the stories go that an entire barbecued cow was consumed, such was the crowd.

Practical joking was a part of the fiesta mood. The early Californians had great fun with cascarónes. These were made with fresh eggs. Tiny holes were poked in each end, and the raw yolk and white were blown out and used for cooking. The empty shells were decorated with intricate wax patterns, then were dipped in dye. Perfumed water or tiny pieces of confetti were placed in the shell before the ends were waxed shut. As the music played and the guests twirled out on the patio, the party-goers would throw these at one another. With any luck, the shell broke and a friend was doused or showered with confetti. This naturally invited retaliation and the cascarónes would fly again!

Courtesy Ralph Rambo

Life wasn't all play, however. John Gilroy became a naturalized Mexican citizen in 1833. Don Ignacio Ortega died in this same year. Governor Figueroa of Mexico, who was presiding at the time, granted all the lands of Rancho San Ysidro, a little over 13,000 acres, to Ortega's three children and their families. Each of them received approximately one square league or 4,460 acres. Son Quentin's share was adjacent to that of Maria Clara and John Gilroy's. Daughter Ysabel's was the northern portion and she and her husband, Julian Cantua, called it Rancho La Polka.

The houses of the two brothers-in-law sat about fifty yards apart. John and Maria Clara's adobe was right near the intersection of the Pacheco Pass Highway and Frazier Lake Road. Sometime when you're out that way, try to picture in your mind these early ranches. They were close to the site where San Ysidro School stands. Life once moved at a much slower pace there, where now a steady stream of traffic rushes by.

Besides raising cattle, Gilroy also grew wheat on his land. There was a grist mill at the ranch which was powered by mules. John Gilroy was also a soap-maker and employed others as well at this trade. Apparently Gilroy was quite intelligent, with a special ability in mathematics. Over the years various neighbors with no talent for figuring called upon Gilroy to help them keep their account books straight.

John Gilroy served as Alcalde (mayor) of San Ysidro for a number of years. In 1846 he was appointed Justice of the Peace (juez de paz) of this district by Commodore Stockton.

Cards and gambling games were a favorite pastime in Rancho days. The game of monte, in which the betting is fast-paced, was one that John Gilroy couldn't resist. Sad to say, he lost a great deal of money to the cards. In order to meet his debts, he had to sell off, parcel by parcel, the rich farmland bequeathed to him and Maria Clara. He received financial assistance in his last years from the British Benevolent Society. Gilroy died penniless in July of 1869 at the age of 75.

He arrived in California more than fifty years before his death with nothing but his spirit of adventure. He died, leaving a fine family, but no fortune to those kinfolk.

His memory lives on here, however. The town which the early settlers called Pleasant Valley became an incorporated city in March of 1870. Gilroy was chosen as its name, in honor of this colorful Scotsman. Gilroy's descendents are many. Mr. and Mrs. Ben Gilroy Senior and Junior continue to make their homes in our community. The younger Gilroy still farms land along the Pacheco Pass Highway, as his ancestors once did.

Other Settlers

The first American to settle here was a man named Doak. In researching, I read of a Thomas Doak who came to our shores at Monterey Bay aboard the whaler *Albatross* in 1816. Doak, who was from Boston, was weary of life at sea and left his ship at this point. He was a carpenter by trade, a block and tackle maker aboard ship.

In 1818, he made his way to the Mission at San Juan Bautista. Having artistic ability, he agreed to paint murals inside the chapel, in exchange for his room and board. He is also credited with painting the fine reredoes (the partitioned wood sculptures behind the altar) which still grace this lovely mission church. Brand of Rancho Las Animas
In 1820, Thomas Doak married Maria Lugarda Castro, daughter of Mariano Castro who was owner of Rancho Las Animas. The couple had six children in all.

Other histories report that the first American here was Philip Doak, who arrived in our valley in 1822. Philip was also a whaler. Seeking a life on terra firma, he too left his ship at Monterey, came to the Gilroy area, and subsequently married a daughter of Mariano Castro. These accounts sounded like the same man, with a few conflicting details.

It turns out that Thomas W. Doak did come to Monterey in 1816, and did leave his ship. Within two years, he was baptized Catholic at the Mission San Juan Bautista. He took as his christening name Felipe (Spanish for Philip) Santiago. Apparently he often went by the name of Philip from that point on, thus explaining our "other" settler! Thomas W. Felipe Santiago Doak and his wife eventually settled on a part of the Rancho Las Animas. Years later, their daughter Maria de la Incarnacion married Nicodemus Gilroy, the oldest son of John and Maria Clara Gilroy.

The third non-Spanish settler in our valley was Mathew Fellom. A Dane, he too was a crewman aboard a whaling ship. He left a life at sea in 1822 when his ship set in along our northern coast, in the Fort Ross vicinity. The following year, he made his way south, eventually arriving in Pleasant Valley. He hired on as a soapmaker, working for John Gilroy. In time, he bought acreage which was part of Rancho San Ysidro. He married Manuela Briones and they raised a large family. Later on, his sons purchased additional sections of the Rancho lands.

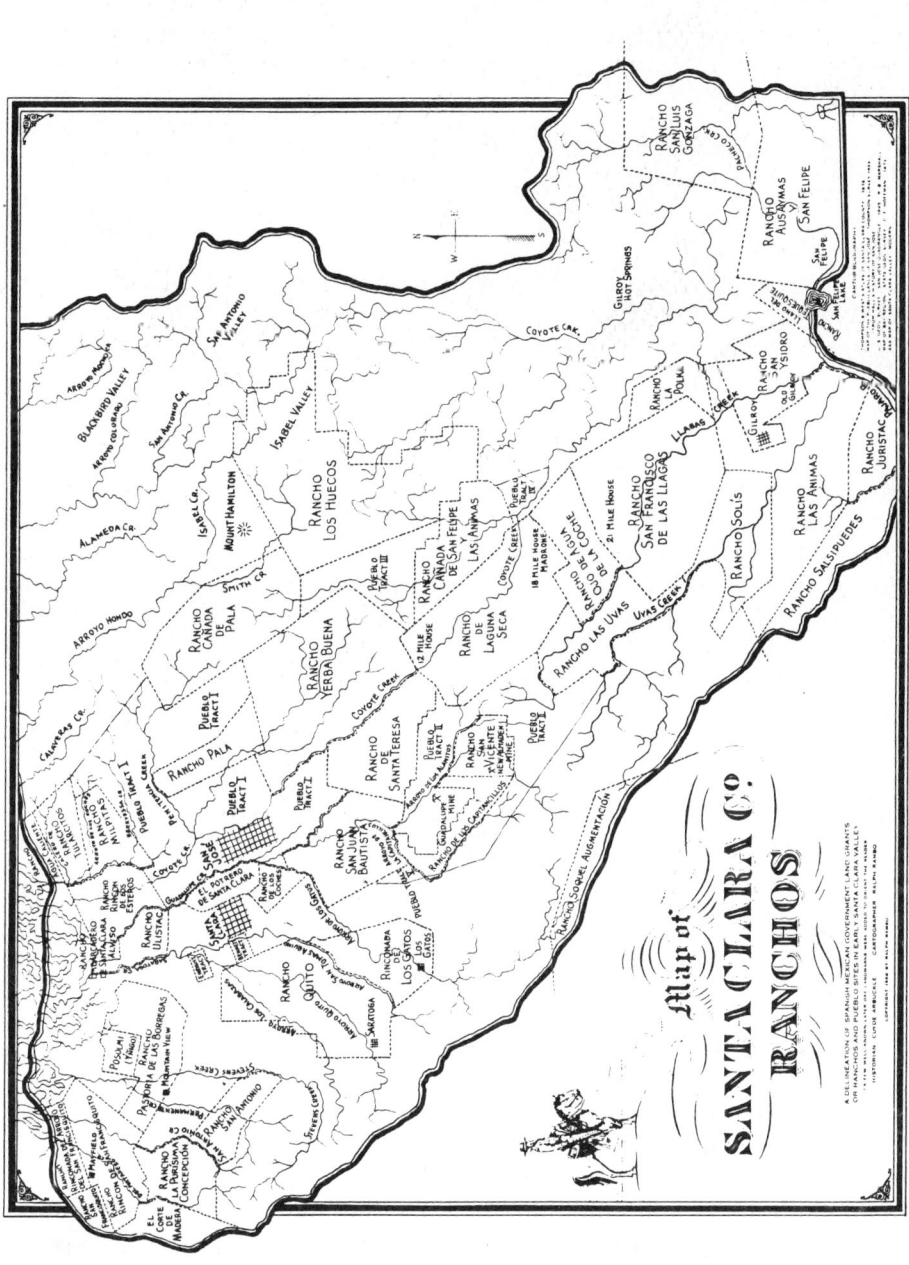

This map researched by historian Clyde Arbuckle and drawn up by Ralph Rambo, gives you an idea of how our county was divided up during the Rancho years.

This house, once the Fellom home, was built in 1861 and is still standing.

Mathew Fellom prospered here. For years he managed the largest livestock business in this area. In 1861, the Felloms built the home pictured here out on the Leavesley Road. It is still standing, and is one of the oldest houses in the Gilroy vicinity. Not long ago, it was added to the Santa Clara County Heritage Resource Inventory. This home remained in the Fellom family until 1957, nearly a century.

* * * * *

It is estimated that by 1830 there were probably only about one hundred "foreigners" in California. If there were many others, we have no written records of them. Of those here, it is assumed all came by vessel, for accounts of overland westward travel date only as far back as 1841. The migration west was mostly to Oregon. Some of the wagon trains, upon reaching the Sierras, would hear reports of California. A few of them did turn southward to find the fertile valleys described. But most continued to their original destination in those "pre-gold" years.

In 1843, Julius Martin came west with a party which included Major S.J. Hensley, Thomas J. Shadden, and Winston Bennett. This was a significant company of travellers, for the wives of Martin, Shadden and Bennett accompanied them, as did Martin's daughters. These were the first "foreign" women on record to settle in our area.

The party had travelled overland with a large train destined for Oregon. Near Fort Laramie, they met Joseph Reddeford Walker who was returning to California as leader of a smaller group. Walker spoke highly of the possibilities in the region to the south of Oregon. Julius Martin and those named above joined the Walker party. Thus they were brought by him across Walker Pass and into the land called California.

Julius Martin settled with his family in San Ysidro, arriving on December 26, 1843. He had travelled west with the equipment needed to construct a mill. This Walker party, probably due to the winter conditions, had to abandon their wagons and everything they couldn't easily carry in the desert just east of Walker Pass. Later, Martin did build a small horse-powered mill in San Ysidro which could turn out twenty bushels a day. The Martin place was across the road from John Gilroy's home. Many years ago, when the ground there was being plowed in preparation for planting, two old millstones were unearthed. It is very likely that they were once a part of Martin's milling system. Awhile later, George White, who was there for the first discovery, found a third. He was leasing land on the old Burchell Ranch for agricultural purposes. Part of the deal with the owner was that he tear down the old home and put two living quarters for field hands in its place. Under one corner of this old building lay the third crude millstone. All three appear to have been fashioned from the lava rock which is found along the lower ridge of our eastern foothills.

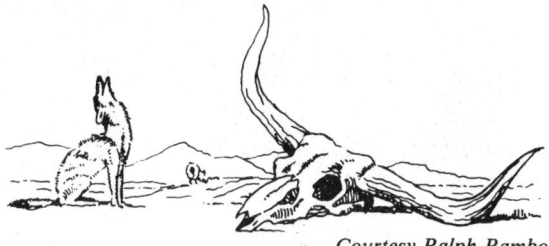
Courtesy Ralph Rambo

Julius Martin was a captain of the American Scouts under Fremont's direction. He was among those present at Sonoma when the Bear Flag was raised on June 14, 1846.

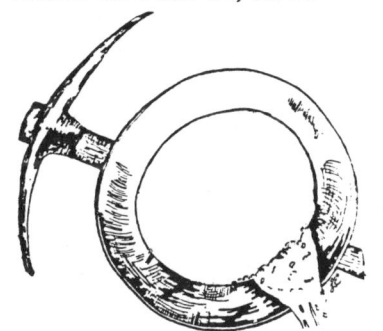

In 1849, Charles Bennett, John Sutter's messenger, stopped briefly in San Ysidro enroute to government headquarters at Monterey to report the discovery of gold at Sutter's Mill. Julius Martin was one of many whose fancy was captured by the tales of the wealth available in "them thar hills". He left shortly thereafter to seek his fortune in the gold fields.

When he returned to San Ysidro in 1850, he had enough money to purchase 1,220 acres of Rancho San Ysidro from John Gilroy. The deed was dated January 8, 1852. Martin kept the property until he died in 1891.

He was blind the last thirty years of his life, but that didn't slow him down. He was a man of good education, and had an excellent memory. In his later years he shared with interviewers his rich recollection of life here in the early years. It is due to Julius Martin that we have a record of many of the people and events which shaped our history in the 1800's.

* * * * *

In 1844, a year after the Julius Martin family settled in our valley, Martin Murphy Sr., who was nearing sixty years of age at the time, arrived from Missouri with his family. He was born in County Wexford, Ireland in 1785, and moved to Canada with his wife Mary Foley Murphy and several of their younger children in 1820. They remained for some years in Canada, until the pioneering spirit of an expanding United States beckoned Murphy. About 1840, the family re-located near St. Joseph, Missouri. It was here that his dear wife Mary and three of their grandchildren succumbed to malaria.

Hearing enthusiastic reports from a priest who had visited California, and feeling the need to leave this place full of sorrowful memories, Murphy set out once again, this time on the long journey across the plains. The Stevens-Murphy-Townsend party, as his unit is often referred to, were the first wagon train of immigrants to cross the Sierra Nevada Mountains. The long trek ended safely in Sacramento.

Martin Murphy Sr. made his way south to our valley, and purchased the Rancho Ojo de Agua de la Coche. There he built an adobe home not far off the El Camino Real, which became a noted spot of warmth and hospitality for miles around.

In those years, there were no established churches here. The closest houses of worship were the Missions to the north in San Jose and Santa Clara, or to the south at San Juan Bautista. Attending a worship service was a full day's journey to and fro for residents of Pleasant Valley. Being a devout Catholic, Martin Murphy sought to remedy this situation. In the early 1850's, Mr. Murphy offered four acres of his land to the Catholic Church for a chapel and a cemetary. The property was near the intersection of Church and New Avenues.

The Archbishop Alemany in San Francisco accepted this generous offer. The little chapel that was built there in the country was the parish church for the Catholics of South County until St. Mary's was founded in 1865. It was named St. Martin's Chapel, after Mr. Murphy's patron saint, St. Martin of Tours. It stood until April of 1877 when it was destroyed by fire. The nearby town of San Martin acquired its name from this source.

Over the years, Martin Murphy purchased other ranchlands. His holdings grew to include approximately 40,000 acres. When this much beloved gentleman died in March of 1865, it was a grievous occasion for all of Pleasant Valley and beyond. The funeral was attended by hundreds of mourners, and the County buildings suspended business for the day. Martin Murphy Sr. is buried in the Catholic cemetary in Santa Clara.

More of Our Valley is Settled

Brand of Rancho La Polka

It was noted earlier that Rancho San Ysidro was divided among Don Ortega's three children and their families. His daughter, Maria Ysabel, you will remember, received the northern portion and called it Rancho La Polka.

In 1849, Ysabel sold this land to Bernard Murphy, son of Martin Murphy Sr. Two years later, Bernard went back to Canada where his family had lived for some twenty years. He brought back to California with him his sister Johanna and his new bride. Bernard and Catherine O'Toole, also of County Wexford were married in Frampton, and then started their life together here in Pleasant Valley. They made the trip west via the Isthmus of Panama, and settled into a pre-fabricated tin house which had been assembled on the Rancho. A big piece of tin from this house is still preserved in the downstairs portion of our Gilroy Museum.

In 1853, Bernard Murphy was killed along with thirty others in a tragic explosion of the boilers aboard the steamboat *Jenny Lind*, which made a regular run between San Francisco and Alviso. Catherine O'Toole Murphy was too soon a widow.

Apparently she was a remarkable woman, possessed of an excellent business sense, which wasn't "expected" of ladies in those days. She proved herself capable of running the operations of what grew to be considerable land holdings. Tragedy struck her life again some years later when her only son, Martin J.C. Murphy, took ill while attending school at Georgetown and died of the fever.

In 1862 she married widower James Dunne, owner of the San Felipe (or Dunne) Ranch and a part of the Topo Ranch. Dunne was also originally from Ireland. Theirs was a good marriage, although he died just twelve years later. Three children were born to the couple. Son Jimmy managed the ranch for many years.

After his death, the O'Connell family leased and then later became owners of this vast ranchland estate which included the lovely home that Jimmy Dunne and his wife Viola built in 1907. In recent years Mr. and Mrs. James O'Connell Jr. have been hard at work restoring the inside of this main house and putting back into the interior decoration many of the original furnishings, fixtures and so forth.

Several years ago the bulk of the Dunne Ranch acreage was sold to a partnership of three Los Gatos-based physicians and a certified public accountant. The partners, ardent horsemen themselves, hope to keep the landscape as it is. The O'Connells retained the house and the acreage around it in the sale. They continue to operate a livestock business in this setting, surely one of the most picturesque in our valley. Their home, known as Casa Del Rancho, is listed in the Santa Clara County Heritage Resource Inventory.

* * * * *

Massey Thomas was another notable settler. Born in Kentucky in 1813, he moved with his family to Missouri in his early teens. There he farmed with his kin until the "gold fever" struck him. He joined a train of forty-two wagons heading for California.

Massey Thomas tried his luck at mining, but realized within a few short weeks that the yellow metal wasn't as easily found as rumors to the Midwest had indicated. An enterprising man, he surmised, that one could be assured of more certain success by catering to the hundreds who were swarming to the gold fields. He took up teaming, and reportedly operated a grocery store for a while as well.

He decided after a year and a half of this type of business that what he was truly comfortable with was farming. And so in early 1851 he returned to Missouri. He stayed only long enough to organize his next move which was to return to California in 1853, driving three hundred head of cattle with him. This was the first such drive. He came directly to the Gilroy area, and settled on land to the southwest of town. Thomas Road runs through acreage which was once the large "Old Homestead" of the Thomas family. A part of this land still belongs to his descendents.

Massey Thomas

Massey Thomas was a successful breeder of fine grazing stock. He raised wheat and barley on a part of his holdings, and also developed extensive orchards. The rich variety of agricultural undertakings on his vast property, carried out in the most scientific methods then known, made his ranch one of the most valuable in the valley.

In all, Massey and his wife Phoebe Bane Thomas, also a native Kentuckian, had ten children. The Thomases were highly regarded by their fellow citizens, as were their kin who followed them. Massey Thomas passed away at his home in 1900 at the age of 87.

His grandson Leon Thomas was at one time a foreman for Henry Miller at the Bloomfield Ranch. He later served as municipal judge of Gilroy from 1931-1959. His gavel is another part of Gilroy's past on display at our Museum. Great-grandsons of Massey Thomas Sr., Jack and Ben Thomas, continue to reside in Gilroy. Their sister, Peggy Thomas Lytle, makes her home in San Jose.

Regrettably, the historic "Old Homestead" on Thomas Road burned to the ground in August of 1979. It was a part of our County Heritage Resource Inventory.

* * * * *

Samuel and Electa Rockwell Ousley brought their family west as part of a train of immigrants in 1852. That fall they stopped in Salt Lake City, Utah where they stayed for the winter. In July of 1853 they arrived in California, settling briefly near Placerville. In March of the following year, they found their way to Pleasant Valley and established a home on land which was part of the Rancho Solis grant. They set to work farming, along what is today the Hecker Pass Highway.

Sketch from 1980 Garlic Festival Program

Tragedy struck the family not long after their arrival here. Samuel was killed while working in a well on a neighboring farm. Electa was left alone in this new territory to carry on the work of the farm, and the raising of the couple's nine children. Of sturdy stock, she faced adversity squarely, and lived to the age of 84.

Clear title to the land she farmed caused troubles for the widow Ousley more than once. In 1879, Electa was a part of the lawsuit, Henry Miller et al (of the Castro heirs) v.s. Massey Thomas et al (of the Sanchez heirs). Uncertainty as to rights of ownership of these acres once a part of the Las Animas and Solis Ranchos grants was the issue. Miller figured those involved could force a decision by the government if they brought it into court. The decision didn't go in Electa's favor, and she had to buy back approximately half of her acreage from Miller. Even with such setbacks, the farm prospered and diversified. Crops produced on the land included such things as orchard fruit, grapes, tobacco, and grains.

In the 1870's the city of Gilroy purchased part of the Ousley Ranch. On that land a municipal reservoir was constructed which served as a storage site for water piped from Uvas Dam for many years.

Beginning in 1925, a portion of the farm was leased to the city for use as a golf course. This came about through an agreement with Mary and Clara Ousley, daughters of Electa and Samuel. Upon Mary's death in 1936, the golf course was given to the city by her heirs as a gift, with the understanding that the land remain a golf course. And so it has . . .the entrance to the Gilroy Golf and Country Club lies only a short distance west of the homestead which for over a century remained the property of the Ousleys and their descendents.

Henry Miller

The name Henry Miller has popped up more than once in our discussion of the early settlers in our valley. Most of you will recognize this man, sometimes referred to as "The Cattle King". Miller Park, Miller Avenue, Bloomfield Ranch, Mt. Madonna . . .all are vestiges of this legendary figure in Gilroy's history.

Born Heinrich Alfred Kreiser in Germany on July 21, 1827, this young man ventured alone to the United States in 1846. Having grown up on a farm, and having gained some knowledge of livestock, he first found work in a butcher shop in New York City. In the year 1848, like it did to so many, the alluring news of gold in California piqued his interest and his desire to move west. Using the ticket and passport of an acquaintance named Henry Miller, he set sail for San Francisco. He travelled via the Isthmus of Panama where he stayed briefly, arriving in San Francisco in 1850.

He soon found employment, again as a butcher. He decided he rather liked his new name, and kept it. Years later it was legally changed by an act of the California State Legislature.

It wasn't long before this enterprising young Henry Miller was in business for himself. Within two years, American cattle were arriving in San Francisco. The Mexican longhorns raised by the Californians were no longer prized, and many ranchers were going under.

Henry Miller

Miller was shrewd enough to know that real and continued success lay in owning his own stock. About this time, Miller observed that some very fine cattle were coming to market, with hides bearing the HH Brand. The Hildreth & Hildreth operation was located on the vast Rancho Sanjon de Santa Rita near Los Banos and encompassed approximately 100,000 acres. Miller's acquisition of a portion of this Rancho was a significant move, for with it came the rights to the HH brand, which in the years to follow marked the left hip of hundreds of thousands of cattle and horses.

Henry Miller's Double H Brand

In 1857, Miller secured options on all the head available north of the Tehachapis, and shortly thereafter entered into a partnership with Charles W. Lux. Thus began the Miller & Lux firm which would eventually amass a grazing empire of over 1½ million acres in three states.

As to how Miller decided on Gilroy for his headquarters, the story goes like this. Prior to the Hildreth & Hildreth purchase, Miller set out on horseback to look over that land. He travelled down the El Camino Real, and eventually up a rough mountain trail which was the start of today's Pacheco Pass Highway. At that time it was the only route through the Coast Range to the San Joaquin Valley. He paused at the summit, and looking back, surveyed the splendor of our tranquil, "Pleasant Valley". Beyond the valley floor rose the Santa Cruz Mountain Range, lush with redwood forests. It is reported that Miller said to himself, "It is a beautiful valley. I must own it." In the ensuing years, he did come to own approximately twenty-five square miles of this valley.

The center of the huge Miller & Lux cattle business was at Bloomfield Ranch, a few miles south of town. A part of this land had been the Rancho Las Animas. In all, Miller purchased some 13,000 acres of this Rancho. Miller was married first to Nancy Sheldon, who died in childbirth, as did the couple's infant son. In 1860, Miller was wed to Sarah Wilmarth Sheldon, the niece of his first wife. Two daughters and a son were born to the couple.

The lovely forty-four room mansion pictured here was built in 1888. Bloomfield was a community within itself, boasting such facilities as its own machine shops, livery stables, blacksmith shop, granaries, poultry houses, a general store, and even a railroad shipping station. After Miller's death in 1916, his widowed daughter-in-law, Sarah Onyon Miller, a Gilroy native, lived on in the mansion for some years. This landmark burned to the ground in June of 1923. Sarah was there at the time of the fire, but escaped uninjured.

The Miller mansion at Bloomfield Ranch south of town was built in 1888.

Not far from the central ranchhouse and grounds was Miller's Glen Ranch, source of the stones used for the exterior of our old City Hall, built in 1905-06.

Miller's favorite spot was the land that he owned in the beautiful redwood forest to the west of town. Mount Madonna was home to Miller--the place where he entertained and relaxed with his family and friends. It was the

This part of Miller's Glen Ranch is still called Indian Camp. Stone from this quarry was used in building the city hall. Notice the "potholes" in the large rocks made by the Indians.

place where he did not conduct business dealings.

The elaborate summer home pictured here was built in 1901, replacing a much smaller redwood cabin constructed before the turn of the century. Smaller bungalows were also erected for family members. Tents were set up when necessary to accommodate overnight guests.

The Miller's "Summer House" atop Mount Madonna was home to the cattle baron. The acreage there included grazing land, orchards, and vineyards.

A visit to this quiet, heavily wooded section of Mt. Madonna Park takes one back in time. Only the bare stone foundations of these once lovely dwellings remain today. As you stand inside these walls, it is not difficult to envision the colored lights in the trees, and the strains of music wafting on a soft evening breeze as Miller's guests whirl around the spacious ballroom floor . . . .

The Ranger Station, the family home of one of Miller's foreman, contains a fine display of photographs and accounts of the various facets of Miller's life. Featured, of course, are the items which capture the grandeur of the festive barbecues and parties at Mount Madonna which were once the pride of Miller hospitality.

Heinrich Alfred Kreiser . . . . Henry Miller . . . . surely one of California's and even the nation's most legendary figures. He arrived in San Francisco with less than ten dollars in his pocket. Yet never before nor since has one man in these United States amassed more land. Lux ran the paperwork part of the business, and Miller spent most of his time on horseback, checking on their various ranches and herds.

Miller was a stickler for detail. Clyde Arbuckle shared with me a case in point, and one of many stories related to him by James (Jimmy) H. Vandiveer who was employed by Miller for sixteen years. Vandiveer frequently accompanied Miller on his "ranch rounds". During a visit to one of them, Miller noted that the workmen doing the butchering were leaving too much meat on the bones. He couldn't tolerate waste and demanded better performance. The next time they were by that same facility, the situation was the same. Vandiveer said Miller fired those men on the spot. "Fortunes are made by the taking care of small things", was a pet expression of Miller's.

Although possessing remarkable business acumen, Miller's personal life was fraught with circumstances over which he had no control. In addition to the loss of his first wife and infant son, his daughter, Sarah Alice, by his second wife, was thrown from her horse at the age of twelve and killed instantly. His son Henry Jr. died in his early 40's, and his dear wife Sarah preceded him in death by ten years.

One cannot help but contemplate the timeless notion of money, power and fame--and whether it is possible to have all of them and happiness besides . . .

Other Firsts

By the mid-1800's the town that was to become Gilroy was growing to the west of the little village of San Ysidro.

James Houck arrived in Pleasant Valley in 1850, having journeyed west from Ohio. He built one of the first houses in what is now the city limits of Gilroy. The building was actually a roadside inn with a stable in back. This establishment served as an overnight resting spot for travellers making their way from Monterey to San Jose. It was located on the Monterey Highway, just north of Lewis Street. The inn was built of sturdy split redwoods, brought down from the forests west of town.

Lucian Everett built the next structure, a trading post type of store on Lewis Street. Eventually, Houck and Everett became business partners. James Houck, who reportedly could neither read nor write, was nonetheless enterprising. He established the first "post office" here. I use quotes because he merely mounted a cigar box on his front porch! Pickup and delivery was not on any regular basis, need we say. We all tend to grumble from time to time about the postal system of today. But in fairness, we must admit that our current facility at Fourth and Eigleberry Streets provides a dependability we should be grateful for!

Courtesy Ralph Rambo

The Gold Rush brought many more pioneers to California in the 1850's. It is not possible to list every one of them here, but all played a part in the growth of our community.

The Fitzgerald family came here from Canada, not because of gold, but because of accounts of another rich resource here, the fertile farmlands. They became active, contributing members of the growing town. Mr. Milton Holsclaw established the first blacksmith shop. John Eigleberry built the first single-family dwelling in the town, on one corner of the intersection of Fourth and Eigleberry Streets.

The first hotel built was originally intended to be a private residence of the David Holloway family. It was constructed in the winter of 1853-54. It was situated along Monterey Highway between Lewis Street and Martin's Lane (now I.O.O.F. Avenue), which was a convenient location for serving the public. And so in 1854 it was converted to provide overnight accommodations to travellers.

The list of newcomers continued to grow. These family names were among them: Bane, Rea, Day, Dowdy, Eschenburg, Rucker, Hanna, Crews and Ferguson. They all sound familiar don't they? All of these early settlers have had a street named after them. If you are interested in learning more details of our pioneers, our Museum has excellent records on many of these families. Numerous personal belongings are displayed there as well. Descendents of these nineteenth century residents have been most generous in donating many family treasures to our Museum.

In addition, you might enjoy doing further research on your own. Many of the texts listed in my bibliography are a part of the library section of our Museum. The books cannot be checked out, but the pleasant atmosphere there makes it a nice place to spend some free time reading. Mary Prien, our Museum Director is knowledgeable on nearly every aspect of Gilroy's history. If she doesn't have a ready answer, she sets to work finding one. I would imagine that many of you have driven past this handsome structure, a former Carnegie Library, at the corner of Fifth and Church Streets and thought, "I'll have to visit there one of these days." Treat yourself--do it!

Another settler of the 1850's I'd like to mention is Horace Willson. A bricklayer by trade, he settled here in 1853. Through experimentation, he found that the natural clay soil here was an excellent base for the making of quality bricks. He perfected his formula in 1854. This same year, he bought a small parcel of land from José Ahumada, land that was close to the Gilroy's spread. The following year he bought approximately forty-two acres of San Ysidro land from John and Maria Clara Gilroy. In 1859 he began construction of this handsome brick home which is located on the Pacheco Pass Highway near the intersection of Frazier Lake Road. Willson's record book has an entry on March 19, 1861, "Moved into new home today."

The brick kiln was right there on the property, about 150 feet from the house. The foundation of the kiln was later used as the base for a charming pergola. Although the pergola or arbor is gone, the brick foundation remains to this day.

Horace Willson was a farmer and cattle rancher as well. In addition to the land he cultivated near his home, his grazing operation in the foothills east of town involved another 20,000 acres. He kept a very complete account book of all his business transactions. His brother Albert's great-grandson, George Willson White, still has this journal. Reading through it gives one a fine insight into the agricultural management processes of a century ago.

The brick home constructed by Horace Willson remains a private residence to this day.

Courtesy Ralph Rambo

Early Schools and the Growth of Our District

We have discussed the fact that many families were settling here, most of them families with young children. The momentous 1850's saw the birth of our school system as well.

Some histories make mention of a one-room schoolhouse built by settlers in San Ysidro village. To our best knowledge, the first classes held in town were in 1852, under the direction of William Reynolds Bane. The early records of our school district were destroyed by a fire in 1867. The information that was reconstructed after that loss came mostly from citizen's memories. Needless to say, the facts vary somewhat. I have tried to outline for you those facts agreed upon by all.

Pictured here is the first public school building that was constructed in town. This facility was built in 1853 on the west side of Church Street, between Third and Fourth Streets. W.R. Bane was one of two trustees for the school. The other was teacher Dempsey Jackson, who taught his four boy pupils (two of them Banes) the 3 R's and also how to shoot!

This is a rare old photograph of our first public school building in Gilroy.
It stood on Church Street between Third and Fourth Streets.

To give you a little more background on our pioneer educator, Bane hailed from Bracken County, Kentucky, where he was born in 1818. You may recall reading the name Bane earlier in our story. Massey Thomas was wed to Phoebe Bane . . .the sister of William Reynolds Bane. It is likely that Mr. Bane came west with the same wagon train as Massey Thomas. Both returned east in 1851 to collect their families, and then return to California.

By some accounts, Bane is credited with building the second single-family dwelling in town. The home was south and east of the present day Bane's Lane, with a driveway off the Lane leading to it. It was in this home that the first Protestant church services were held, which you'll hear more about later.

W.R. Bane served on the city council from 1878-1880. He was then elected to the high school board, and served on that committee for a number of years.

Records on this family are sketchy. Bane and his wife, the former Ann Woods Brown, had ten children in all, it is thought. Mr. Bane died in Oakland in 1893, but was brought to Gilroy and laid to rest in the large family plot. The Bane property became a part of Henry Miller's land holdings, and later was purchased by Henry Brem. The house has been gone for many years now.

*****

For a long while all the grades in the public school, kindergarten through twelfth grade, could be taught in the same building. However, by 1872 high school classes were conducted in a separate building. William Finley was the first high school principal. Classes met in the Methodist Episcopal Church building. When the church convention was held locally, the youngsters had time off from lessons. It should also be mentioned that in the early 1860's Sarah Severance built and managed a private school for girls on Railroad Street, known as The Miss Sarah M. Severance Seminary.

In addition, the Catholic School, whose location at that point in time was described as being one-half mile north of the center of town, was founded in 1870. "The Convent proper," as it was titled in *Gilroy School History 1853-1888*, compiled by Eugene F. Rogers, "where young women received their instructions was then under the direction of Sister Superior Ramanda Cremadell." Mr. Rogers was City Clerk for years, and an employee of the *Gilroy Gazette*. This interesting little booklet was published in 1888 by the *Gazette*. Rogers went on to relate that in 1877, Catherine Dunne gave $5,000 for the building and maintaining of a school for boys. This institution of learning was constructed directly south of the Convent proper. Her stipulation was that no boys over the age of fourteen were to attend. Approximately fifty boys at one time were students there. Mr. Rogers also reported that these schools shared the resources of a fine music department, which included two pianos.

St. Mary's Parochial School continues to this day to provide a fine educational program for the youngsters of South County enrolled there.

Nine public schools were listed in the Gilroy area as of this 1888 summary. The countryside was divided into elementary districts, which operated independently, each having its own schoolhouse and teacher. Besides the school on Church Street, the following existed at that time: San Ysidro, Adams, Live Oak, Mt. Dell, Redwood, Carnadero, Hot Springs, and Rhodes. Rucker School to the north of town was established in 1894. Nearly all of these schools are gone now. With the coming of modern transportation earlier in this century, the students from rural areas were bused to schools more centrally located. Two country schools are still a part of Gilroy's educational system, San Ysidro and Rucker. Both of these schools became a part of the Gilroy Unified School District in 1966. Our other elementary schools today include Eliot, Las Animas, Glen View, El Roble, and Jordan which shares a campus with the Brownell Fundamental School.

Gilroy's first high school building was also located on Church Street between Third and Fourth Streets.

It was in 1898 that the first high school building was constructed. Pictured here, this institution was also situated on Church Street between Third and Fourth Streets. In 1912, a new high school was built on I.O.O.F. Avenue. The original campus then became the site of the Severance School. The 1912 high school facility was replaced in the 1950's, and this newer campus served our city until 1978. Today, as you know, this is the location of South Valley Junior High School. The present-day campus for Gilroy High School is at the corner of Tenth and Princevalle Streets.

Our School Administration Building is located in the same block which housed our first schools. Mt. Madonna High School shares a part of this land. Although our first high school no longer stands, the bell which resounded from the tower (seen in the middle of the roof) is the same one mounted in-front-of the Administration Building. The little plaque

underneath tells of its history. This bell also became our district's logo. Take note of it sometime when you're walking in that area. Another treasure that was part of our first high school is the square piano, purchased with funds raised by students and parents. Still in fine condition, it may be viewed in the downstairs section of the Gilroy Museum.

I'd also like to make mention of an eight-page monthly newspaper which was put out by the district, and called *The Gilroy Public Effort*. It began publication in 1875, and was one of the first of its kind on the Pacific Coast. Contributors included students, teachers, and principals. The students worked with their instructors, learning composition technique and lay-out. The district had its own printing equipment. Local businessmen advertised in this paper, making it self-supporting. It was a fine way for students to share school and local news. Additionally, they were exposed to world events. When you consider how small a city Gilroy was at that time, I think it's remarkable that this kind of opportunity was available for the youngsters. One fragile, yellowed copy of the *Effort* is on file at our Museum.

* * * * *

Professor Elmer E. Brownell

Over the years Gilroy has had the good fortune to have many fine educators as a part of its growing school system. This is still true today. One such person was Professor Elmer E. Brownell. He came to our city in 1904. He was first a teacher, and then for many years the principal of our Public Schools. He also served frequently on committees at the County level, ever working toward the bettering of our educational programs. The school on Carmel Street was named in his honor.

Another educator who deserves special mention is Edward H. Towner. Mr. Towner was the Band Director and head of all instrumental music in the Gilroy schools from February 1931 until June of 1945. Many of you will remember this man.

Edward H. Towner was born in England and made his way to Gilroy during the Depression years. With money scarce and unemployment high, many of the school programs were severely trimmed. The Gilroy schools had almost no musical education offered at that time. Edward Towner sensed this lacking, and set to work to change it.

From all accounts, he was a strict teacher, but every student I've heard speak of him, remembers this man fondly. He practiced a kind of "tough love" fifty years ago! He was an excellent musician, specializing in the trumpet. He shared not only his musical talents, but also his abilities to develop a fine marching unit of the youngsters he taught. Gilroy's population was between two and three thousand in the 1930's and 1940's. Nevertheless, this Music Man thought big! A Band Booster's Club was begun in 1935 which helped raise funds for the band to travel to various competitions. Gilroy High School won both state and regional top honors for many years running. A number of individual students also brought home trophies for outstanding solo performances.

Gilroy's Music Man, Edward H. Towner.
Photograph taken in 1936, during the Band's heyday.

Mr. Towner had to resign from his post in 1945 due to failing eyesight. However, he formed another group called The Eagles Band, which was comprised of his former students. Many years ago, an Eagles Band Fund was established. The musicians would contribute a percentage of their earnings for playing at various dances and programs to this fund. These monies have been in the bank since those band days.

In the spring of 1981, members of that Eagles Band decided on a fitting way to put the money into circulation. They changed the name to The Edward H. Towner Memorial Scholarship Fund, and now each June music awards will be given to the most promising instrumentalists in Gilroy. Howard Smith, one of the founders of this program, emphasizes that all ages may apply for a scholarship. The Gilroy Historical Society is the administrator of the Fund. The money is to be used to advance a student's musical education. The student may be six or sixty! Anyone may contribute to this worthwhile project.

Mr. Towner's students are still grateful for the wonderful education he gave to them. They hope, in some way, to enrich the lives of others seeking to develop their own musical skills. If you play an instrument, perhaps you'll give some thought to this fine opportunity which is open to you. There is more information on this, and also a fine exhibit of the band's big years assembled by Ken "Spuds" Taylor in our Gilroy Museum. Mr. Towner's trumpet is also on display there.

Gilroy High School's award-winning band of 1935-36.

The First Churches

Earlier we learned of the first Catholic chapel in our valley, St. Martin's, and of how that led to the eventual establishment of our St. Mary's Church. Let's look now at the beginnings of other denominations in Gilroy.

The first Protestant services were held in 1852, in the home of Mr. and Mrs. William Reynolds Bane. A circuit rider minister of the Methodist Episcopal South Church led those worship services. A Methodist Episcopal congregation was also begun in Gilroy shortly afterward. These churches were completely separate from one another until 1917 when a national merger took place. The new facility these congregations built together at the corner of Fourth and Church Streets was razed by fire in 1938. With faith and determination, the parishoners quickly recovered from their loss. In 1939 they erected and dedicated the mission-style building which still stands on this corner, now the United Methodist Church.

The congregation of the Christian Church was formed in 1855. The Christian Church building on Fifth Street, constructed in 1857, is believed to be the oldest building in the city limits of Gilroy, and the oldest frame church in continuous use in Santa Clara County. You'll notice on the 1885 map that it was originally located on Third Street at Church. It was moved about 1886-87 to its present location when the land on which it first stood was redeeded, as part of the outcome of the Miller et al v.s. Massey Thomas et al title dispute we reviewed earlier.

In May of 1981 this building was nominated for the National Register of Historic Places. Briefly, if you are not familiar with this, the Register is a listing of those places in our nation with special historical significance. Placement on the list not only helps to assure that the structure will be spared the wrecker's ball, but it makes available federal grant monies, to be used for restoration and maintenance purposes.

St. Stephen's Episcopal Church,
the early building

The early building for St. Mary's
Church faced Monterey Street

The Christian Church,
our city's oldest,
was built in 1857

The early Methodist
Episcopal Church

Gilroy's Presbyterian
Church was built in 1869

    This Christian Church has been home to the Lirio Del Valle De Las Asamblas De Dios congregation since 1976. Its members are currently involved in the renovation of this historic house of worship.

    The Presbyterian Church was organized in 1859-60. Their first meeting place was in the Old Gilroy area. The Church at the corner of Fifth and Church Streets was built in 1869. It is the second oldest of all the Presbyterian Church buildings in California. Additions have been made to the structure several times in this century, but the exterior of the sanctuary section and the bell tower have retained their nineteenth century charm.

The Protestant Episcopal Church formed a congregation in the late 1860's. In 1869 a Protestant Episcopal Mission was founded. It served the church in Gilroy, as well as churches of this denomination in communities further south and east. In 1871, St. Stephen's was built at the corner of Martin and Forest Streets. St. Stephen's Episcopal Church is now located at the intersection of Wayland Lane and Broadway.

Mention should also be made of the San Felipe Church, now nestled in the rolling hills of our Gavilan College campus. It was built in 1893 at the corner of Shore Road and Fry Lane in the San Felipe district, San Benito County. In 1972 it was moved to the college and restored as a student project. In 1978 this excellent restoration job received the County Historical Heritage Commission's Preservation Award. This quaint chapel is chosen by many couples for their marriage ceremonies.

Today Gilroy rejoices in having nearly thirty different churches in its midst. Many of them are relatively new to our city. But all of them are involved in outreach programs, striving to meet the needs of people in our community as well as serving our neighbors around the world.

Subdivisions in Pleasant Valley?

James C. Zuck came here as a young man in 1853, having traversed the plains with his family by wagon train. He studied at Santa Clara University where he earned his law degree.

In the fall of 1867 he began the first legal practice in Pleasant Valley.

In 1867, F.S. Rogers opened the first office for the practice of dentistry in town. The building where Rogers practiced had two offices. Lawyer Zuck occupied the other half.

Zuck and Rogers became partners soon after, and went into the real estate business. They acquired five acres in the northwest part of town, and broke it into lots which they sold. Another twenty acres along Monterey Street near the town's center were purchased from John Eigleberry and similarly divided. Later W. L. Hoover joined the firm which then became Zuck, Rogers & Hoover. These men not only went on to create more residential lots, but they also planned the streets for many parts of town.

James Zuck was elected to the State Senate in 1879. In 1881, he departed for Tientsin, North China where he served as a U.S. Consul.

Timber!

Another name that was listed previously and needs to be reviewed in depth is that of William Hanna. Born in Indiana in 1812, he was a farmer and stockman in Illinois for some twenty-six years before he brought his family west. He, his wife Rebekah Cresswell Hanna, and their children made the trip via the Isthmus of Panama, and arrived in San Francisco in January of 1860.

They headed south to Gilroy immediately, where William's brothers Green, Samuel and James were engaged not only in cattle raising and farming, but also in the lumbering business. The brothers had all come overland in the 49er rush, settling in Gilroy after a few years at the mines.

We have talked so much of construction, and it was indeed Gilroy's fortune to have the abundant redwood forests to her west. The oak-dappled valley floor could prosper in part because of the wealth of building material nearby. Remember that Bernard and Catherine Murphy lived in an imported pre-fabricated tin house, as did many others who established themselves here before our timber resource was tapped.

William Hanna claimed to be the first with a logging and a milling operation in the redwoods. In the very early 1860's Hanna sold this part of his business to George Bodfish. Like so many others, Bodfish, a southerner, came to California in the Gold Rush. Bodfish did not keep the mill for long, and passed it on to a relative Orlando Bodfish. In September of 1864 Orlando Bodfish sold to an A.J. Spencer. Although the mill passed through the Bodfish family in a relatively short period of time, the name stuck. The creek that runs through the mountains there was named after this family. For years the main road west out of Gilroy was called the Bodfish Mill Road. Many oldtimers still refer to it this way.

Lumber! Lumber!
WILLIAM HANNA,
Church Street, bet. 6th and 7th.   GILROY, CAL.

Is prepared to furnish all kinds of

LUMBER, BUILDING FINISH,
Doors, Window Sash and Frames,
OF EVERY VARIETY.
STAIR BUILDING,
Turning and Scroll Sawing, with Mouldings
OF EVERY DESCRIPTION.

In 1869 William Hanna built the Gilroy Planing Mill in town. Then in the very early 1870's, partners Lyttleton A. Whitehurst and Pleasant Hodges took over the holdings along the Bodfish Creek. Not long after that they bought the planing mill from Hanna.

His lumbering days past, William Hanna turned to public service. He sat on our first town council, and after incorporation was a member of the first city council. He was Gilroy's mayor from 1876-78, and was elected to serve in the state legislature also during that period.

This 1880's photograph shows the Whitehurst and Hodges lumber mill which operated a thriving business along the Bodfish Creek in the mountains west of town.

William and Rebekah's son Jacob married Clara Rea, daughter of Thomas Rea, a noted dairyman in this valley. The couple moved to Texas for a while to raise cattle. They were the parents of Walter J. Hanna who, though born in Texas, returned to Gilroy as an infant. Later, a graduate of the University of California, he served as Gilroy's city engineer from 1936-56. Upon retirement, his son Walter J. Hanna Jr. took over the position. Another son, William Sandoe Hanna, lives in Gilroy too. Son Edward R. Hanna makes his home in Hollister, and a daughter, Clara May Hanna Lundy resides in Bakersfield. The William Hanna home still stands on the west side of Eigleberry Street, near the corner of Seventh Street.

* * * * *

The Whitehurst & Hodges lumber mill was expanded and continued to do a thriving business for several decades. Roofing shingles and shakes were made in large quantities in addition to millions of board feet of timber. The logs were hauled into town on big wagons pulled by work horses. The horses wore bells on their bridles to warn other travellers that a heavy load was on its way downhill. Vivian Head, born in Gilroy in 1892, recalls that the sound of the bells was a part of the natural rhythm of everyday life for years.

The lumber was planed and finished at the mill and yard in town. Able to complete all phases of the business themselves, Whitehurst and Hodges dominated the local market, and were major suppliers to growing communities throughout the state.

Mr. Whitehurst, it should be added, became very active in local politics. He served two terms on the city council, was city treasurer at one time, and presided as mayor from 1892-94. He was elected to the California State Senate on the Republican ticket.

Gradually, as one would surmise, there were fewer and fewer trees to cut. The mill site was relocated more than once to facilitate the processing of felled timber. Fires plagued the business as well. The logging mill burned in 1904, and in August of 1914, the planing mill on Church Street, between Sixth and Seventh Streets also suffered extensive damage by fire. Although both were rebuilt, these losses were economic setbacks which forecast the eventual demise of the logging industry in our area.

Today many a home stands in Gilroy, made of local redwood. Owing to redwood's qualities of being termite and rot resistant, these buildings are in remarkable shape even though many of them have passed the century mark.

Although there are movements afoot at present to restore limited timber harvesting in our mountains, for now the sounds of logging are silent in our redwoods forests.

Pleasant Valley Becomes the City of Gilroy

We've already touched on some of those who served in local public offices. Let's review at this point just how Gilroy became a city.

The town was growing rapidly, and by the late 1860's the community leaders deemed it the proper time to become well-managed. The town was incorporated in February of 1868. Soon afterward, the first election to determine town officers was held. Then in March of 1870 an act was passed by the California state legislature which made Gilroy a city. This formal declaration brought with it a city charter and a government headed by a mayor, a marshal, a clerk, a treasurer, a city council, and an ex-officio tax collector and assessor.

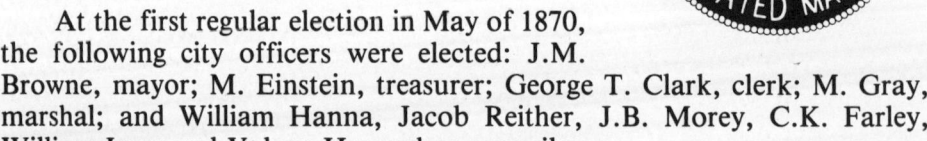

At the first regular election in May of 1870, the following city officers were elected: J.M. Browne, mayor; M. Einstein, treasurer; George T. Clark, clerk; M. Gray, marshal; and William Hanna, Jacob Reither, J.B. Morey, C.K. Farley, William Issac and Volney Howard as councilmen.

Our early officials planned well and with foresight. One thing they strived hard to gain for Gilroy was railroad access. It was a well-known fact that if the trains came through your city, it meant the growth of business, communication, and, of course, better public transportation.

On April 12, 1868 ground was broken in San Jose for the extension south of a connecting railroad line. It was called the Santa Clara & Pajaro

Gilroy's early train depot was located on south Monterey Street as is the present one.

Valley Railroad Company. Upon its completion the following year, the whole town turned out with cheers and band music to welcome the first train which was pulled by three locomotives.

Whether it's to your joy or disgruntlement, the trains still come through Gilroy, but our old depot on South Monterey Street has been closed for many years now. A group within our local A.A.U.W. began the campaign to "stop the train" again in Gilroy. Now a project of the Gavilan Forum, this group is lobbying to restore passenger/commute service to our city. The conductor's call of "All aboard!" may again ring out in Gilroy on a regular basis.

Hotels in Gilroy

The coming of the railroad brought the need for more hotels in Gilroy. The William's House was built in or about 1869, and later became the Central Hotel. It stood on Monterey Street where the parking lot adjacent to J.C. Penney's is today. The Railroad House was built in the winter of 1871-1872. Not long after these overnight resting places were constructed in town, another new hotel was built in the country.

The Gilroy Hot Springs Hotel in our eastern foothills was built by George Roop and his partners, and was completed in 1874. The Hot Springs played a very colorful role in the history of Gilroy. They are located in what is known as the Mount Hamilton Spur of our Coast Range Mountains. If you've ever visited Coyote Lake Park, you travelled there on Roop Road.

The Central Hotel was at first called the Williams House. This was a popular one along Monterey Street in the early days.

The Springs are several miles past the lake, but the road in is no longer open to the public.

The Springs were discovered in 1865. History records give us more than one discoverer's name. Francisco Cantua is one credited with the find, and Ignacio and José Ortega are the other two. The Springs are situated on what was once the outskirts of Rancho San Ysidro land. You may recall these last names from your earlier reading. Researchers aren't positive because written records on this are scanty. But these men may very well have been related to the original Rancho family. Remember that John Gilroy married Maria Clara Ortega, and Maria Clara's sister Ysabel was wed to Julian Cantua.

Speculation aside, the Hot Springs land was sold to George Roop in October of 1866. He began at once to clear a road in, and to build cabins there. Charles Twombly soon became a partner, and the men opened for business the following year.

The resort grew to include the large hotel pictured here. This fine establishment had three dining rooms, and could accommodate approximately 170 overnight guests. The hotel served local products in its dining areas such as butter, cheese, eggs, beef and milk. These items were of such excellent quality that guests apparently urged others to vacation here, to partake of these delights. There were eventually eighteen cottages scattered throughout the grounds which were rental favorites for families. Bathing pools and bath houses were provided, there being separate facilities for men and women.

The mineral waters of the Springs were believed to have actual healing powers. Even today they gurgle out of the ground at an average temperature of 107 degrees. These waters were said to help ease the pain of rheumatism, arthritis, kidney and liver troubles, gout, and so forth. The mud baths were also considered to be excellent for one's health.

A drinking type of fountain was placed over the main spring. Pictured here is that fountain and the kiosk which was built over it to provide shade. The little shiny squares you see at the base of the V-shaped support beams are dippers. A number of them hung around the kiosk. At any time, resort guests could reach into the cistern and scoop out a ladle full of drinking water. I doubt that current health department codes would allow this type of "self-service" nowadays!

The Hot Springs Resort was the place to go for many vacationers. The Southern Pacific had special runs which brought trainloads of San Francisco and Oakland residents down to the Gilroy depot. A wagon would meet the train and transport the guests to the resort grounds. Hugo Hornlein remembers well driving the four horse team to and fro at the ripe old age of sixteen. By 1900 a Stanley Steamer type of "stagecoach" replaced the horse-drawn wagon.

Recreation was superb at the Hot Springs. Besides swimming, guests could enjoy pastimes like shuffleboard, croquet, and various card and board games. There were many scenic hiking and riding trails nearby. Coyote Creek afforded good fishing, and hunting in the surrounding hills was also good. A spacious dancefloor out under a woodland canopy was the setting for popular evening entertainment, as guests danced to the music of live bands.

In 1905, the William McDonald family became the managers of the resort, and for awhile in the years to follow, they were owners.

In 1938, Japanese-American Henry Sakata purchased the property. For a time business picked up, as Sakata successfully promoted this scenic area as a perfect spot for picnicking.

The resort was closed down during World War II. During the 1950's the Kato family were proprietors, and again accommodated mostly picnickers. Volleyball, hiking, swimming and horseback riding were also offered.

In 1963 the buildings were condemned for public use. The two hundred forty or so acres have been privately owned by a large number of investors since 1964. This group has made several attempts to determine the feasibility of reestablishing the resort. The major stumbling block is the sewage treatment facility. To date, none of the proposed systems has met with the County's approval. The worst blow to the project's progress came in the early morning hours of September 7, 1980. Trespassers into the grounds started a fire which quickly spread through a major portion of the resort proper. Destroyed were the over 100-year-old hotel, the clubhouse, and five of the nearby buildings. This once grand and glamorous setting in Gilroy's history is now just a memory.

Still . . . the warm water continues to flow from the springs. The sturdy kiosk maintains its vigil on the grounds which are richly carpeted with oak

The kiosk shades the main drinking fountain even today. The spacious hotel burned to the ground in September of 1980. Bottom: The warm mineral baths attracted many visitors.

Guests of the resort were picked up at the train depot and driven to the hotel grounds in our eastern foothills in this "taxi".

leaves. Perhaps someday a "stage" will once again carry laughing visitors to this lovely site in our eastern foothills. It's certainly nice to contemplate . . .

The Redwood Retreat

Charles Sanders came west in the 49er rush, all the way from his native Nova Scotia. He spent over a decade in the gold fields, and then returned home to marry Annis Hilton in 1861. Within a short time, he was back in California, searching for a bonanza again. About 1870 he resigned himself to the fact that he was not able to make his living as a miner. By this time, the couple had two sons, Wilburn and Irville.

At this point the family came to our valley where Charles Sanders homesteaded a large tract of land in the mountains west of town. Not long after they'd arrived here, a daughter was born to the couple. Sadly, Mrs. Sanders died in childbirth. The infant girl was named Annis after her mother. The Indian women at Henry Miller's place at nearby Mt. Madonna cared for the baby until she was a toddler. With this assistance, the bereaved family was able to carry on.

Charles and his sons cleared away a large wooded section, and set to work farming this land. Their acreage was planted in vineyards, orchard, and hay and grain crops in addition to a large vegetable garden.

In 1891, the Sanders men completed the Redwood Retreat hotel building pictured here, and opened for business. The hotel could accomodate forty-four overnight guests. In addition, there were a number of rustic cabins scattered in the surrounding woods, which could be rented for extended lengths of time. Many San Francisco businessmen would send their wives and children down for the entire summer, joining them on weekends. The grounds included a large swimming pool and tennis courts. There were miles of beautiful hiking trails all around, and dances were held in a converted prune shed on the weekends.

Over the years, Irville and Wilburn built their own homes on the property and raised their families at the Retreat. Irville and his wife ran the resort. Wilburn and his family tended to the farming of what became an approximately 200 acre estate.

Advertisement from the *Gilroy Advocate*, June 22, 1928.

Leland Sanders, Wilburn's son, recalls that on the Fourth of July of 1908, a fire started in the kitchen of the main hotel building. A blind man was a guest that night and his room was over the kitchen. He was the first to smell the smoke. He aroused his companion and the two men swiftly spread a verbal alarm throughout the hotel. All forty-four occupants escaped unharmed, but the structure was a total loss.

The Sanders rebuilt immediately, but this time their facility was only a clubhouse type of structure. A large living room with a fireplace, a dining room, and a kitchen made up the Retreat center. No hotel rooms were included. The cabins were the only overnight accommodations from that point on.

Before the turn of the century, Fannie Stevenson, the wife of author Robert Louis Stevenson, bought forty acres of land from the Sanders family. She had a home built there in the lush, secluded woods, and called her place "Vanumanutagi", which means, "Vale of the singing birds". Wilburn Sanders was her foreman for years. She would write to him from various parts of the world, telling him when she planned to return to Gilroy. Wilburn would drive her surrey down to the depot and await her train.

Author Frank Norris also bought acreage from the Sanders. A close friend of the Stevenson's, his log cabin was not far from "Vanumanutagi". He had hopes of writing future novels in this tranquil setting, but his sudden death in 1902 at the age of thirty-two shattered those dreams. His cabin was placed on the National Register of Historic Places in 1963. Fannie Stevenson had Wilburn Sanders build a small monument to her friend there in the redwoods. It is a curved bench made of stones, and the inscription reads "Frank Norris 1870-1902 — Simpleness and Gentleness and Humor and Clean Mirth".

Irville Sanders suffered a fatal heart attack after fighting a large forest fire which swept through the mountains around the Retreat in 1917. Following his death, the resort was leased to several different proprietors through the Twenties, and was finally closed during the Depression. The property is still in the family, belonging now to Mrs. Charles Pond of San Jose. Her husband, now deceased, was the son of Annis Sanders Pond, Irville and Wilburn's younger sister.

Leland Sanders related a touching story about his grandfather's last wishes. Charles Sanders is buried in the family cemetary, there on his homesteaded land. He wanted his tombstone to be cut from the craggy red granite rock which was a part of the landscape of his family's farmland in Nova Scotia. Certainly no simple task — but after his death, his sons arranged with relatives back home, and a large chunk of this very rock was shipped to San Francisco, via Cape Horn. From that crude material, a handsome, red granite tombstone was carved. Charles Sanders rests in peace, his wish fulfilled. His son Wilburn, who tended the family land for so many years is at rest there too.

Many of the resort buildings remain standing to this day, although it has been decades since any guests vacationed at the gracious Redwood Retreat.

Our Early Fire Fighters

Regrettably, you have read numerous times in our story of fine places that were destroyed by fires. The early townspeople realized that a fire fighting unit was needed. In July of 1869, the first group organized for this purpose and called themselves The Viligant Engine Company. Two years later they joined forces with another team of volunteers who went by the name of The Eureka Hook & Ladder Company.

The first fire fighters headquarters was on Old Gilroy Street. By 1873, one hundred fifty volunteers were a part of Gilroy's fire department. In 1879, still another group, The Neptune Hose Company, consolidated its equipment and men with the first group. These united fire fighters then changed their name to The Eureka Hook & Hose Company. For a time, the "firehouse", makeshift though it was, was located on Monterey Street between Fifth and Sixth Streets.

We know fire fighting is a perilous, demanding task. But in the early days it was particularly strenuous because the hoses and water tanks had to be pulled to the fire by the volunteers themselves. The various hose cart teams took great pride in maintaining the speed and efficiency of their unit. Fire drills were a source of good-natured, but nonetheless serious competition amongst the teams.

One of Gilroy's "Hose Cart" teams was taking part in a Fourth of July Parade on Monterey Street in the early 1900's when this photo was taken.

You can see one of the teams here, outfitted and ready for action. It had to be a frustrating business back then. No matter how hard the men tried, getting to a fire scene, encumbered and on foot, meant precious time was lost. Often a building was completely engulfed in flames before the fire fighters could reach the scene.

Still, it was a beginning, and as technology progressed, and motorized vehicles came into being, fire protection improved. The fine old brick firehouse at 55 Fifth Street was built in 1916 by William Radtke Sr., and served Gilroy until 1978. The photograph shows you some of the four wheeled units of the 1920's, and you can also see the bell tower atop the firehouse, from which the clanging alarms were sounded. This structure has been remodeled, and now houses a restaurant, Station 55. The old brass sliding pole is still in place, and owner/chef Stan Roberts has worked very hard to achieve an atmosphere with a sense of the valiant past of our city's fire fighting forces.

Our old firehouse on Fifth Street, in about 1920. Notice the shiny wheeled rigs, pride of the force, and the bell tower, now gone.

Our fire department is now headquartered on Wren Avenue at the corner of Welburn Avenue. Our firemen should be commended, not only for their efficiency, but for the many hours they spend in public relations work. Groups of young children learning first-hand about a fireman's job and fire safety are not an uncommon sight at this newest facility. Those of us living outside the city limits are equally grateful for the dedicated service offered by our Rural Fire Department.

The Music Hall.....................The Opera House

As Gilroy continued to grow another need was recognized. The townspeople wished to have a large hall or auditorium for social and cultural events.

In the spring of 1874 a committee formed, and shortly thereafter they issued stock which the citizens were urged to purchase. By this "shares" method, the funds were raised, nearly $7,000, to build what was at first called The Music Hall. In later years it was more prestigiously referred to as The Opera House.

The building was constructed by William Hanna, and stood on the southeast corner of Eigleberry and Fifth Streets. From the street level a short flight of steps led up to the main entrance to the hall. The structure measured forty-eight feet in width and had a depth of eighty feet. At the rear of this spacious room was a large stage which was forty-two feet across the arch and twenty feet deep. The area under the stage was utilized for dressing rooms as well as for storage. There was a gracious anteroom or lobby, and at either end of this lobby were stairways providing access to the gallery or balcony. The balcony contained seating for 180. The entire hall could accommodate 750 people. All of the downstairs seating was moveable so that the room could be cleared for dances or sporting events. One of the fine old wooden benches that was a part of this portable furniture was donated to the city years ago by Mr. and Mrs. George Rianda. It was at the Museum for a time. Now it is "back in circulation" providing seating for cultural events once more, as a part of the furnishings at the Theatre Angels House on Fifth Street.

Looking up Fifth Street from Monterey Street, the old Music Hall is on the left in the background. Photograph taken about 1900.

A myriad of activities were held in this hall over the years. Travelling shows appeared on its stage as well as local talent programs. Political rallies were conducted under its roof. And for a period of time, when no gymnasium existed on campus, the Gilroy High School basketball team played their games in the hall on Saturdays. The local musicians who then called themselves the Gilroy Band held their Grand Ball gala at the Music Hall on more than one occasion. Plays were performed for enthusiastic audiences as well.

This is a look at the interior of the Music Hall when it was decorated for a Republican political rally in 1896.

In 1905, a concert was presented there, sponsored by the Presbyterian Church, where for a short time Rev. Dr. Thomas J. MacMurray was pastor. The concert featured guest violinist Frederick MacMurray, Rev. MacMurray's son. When Frederick presented another concert in 1910, Vivian Moore (Barshinger Head) was a guest soprano as a part of that program. Many of you will remember her. Mrs. Head taught in Gilroy schools for many decades, later becoming the choral music director for our district. Incidentally, if you've wondered . . . yes, this guest violinist was a relation of television and film star Fred MacMurray. This distinguished musician was his father, and the pastor his grandfather. The programs for Frederick MacMurray's Gilroy engagements are in our Museum files, one of them loaned to the Museum by Mrs. Head.

In the winter of 1908, Charles Holmes leased the Music Hall for a five year term. He made several improvements about the hall and stage area. It was under his management that the Music Hall hereafter became known as The Gilroy Opera House.

By the early 1920's Gilroy had the fine Strand Theatre on Monterey Street, which we'll discuss in detail later. The Opera House was no longer the favored spot for large social events. For a time, the hall was the meeting place of our American Legion Post 217.

The building was demolished in the mid 20's, and the Legion built their new facility on that site. The Legion has since moved to the southeast corner of Sixth and Eigleberry Streets, but their old headquarters on Fifth Street still stands.

As with so many parts of our city's history, no trace remains of the building that was once a source of great pride to her citizens, Gilroy's Music Hall . . .Opera House.

The Agricultural Industry . . . . Neighbors from Other Lands

I once read somewhere that the United States is not really a melting pot, as it's so often referred to, where each one's identity gets lost in the mixture. Rather, it is hopefully more like a full salad bowl, where each element maintains its individuality, while still being a part of a varied, rich whole.

Our country, and certainly our valley, have grown and prospered on a foundation of the fine ideas and the back-breaking work of all kinds and colors of people. On many occasions it has been noted that newcomers first came to California to seek gold. Many, we observed, ultimately found that the richest bounty to be had in the golden west was in her fertile soil and mild climate.

From France

One pioneer in agriculture was Louis Pellier. He made his way to our shores from his native France by sailing around Cape Horn. Like hundreds of others, he headed first to the gold fields, but before long was disenchanted with the mining life.

He came to the Santa Clara Valley and settled on farmland in the San Jose area. There, in addition to farming, he also started a nursery and sold trees to other farmers. He quickly realized that the growing conditions here were very similar to those of his homeland, and this gave him an idea.

His brother Pierre was venturing home to France to marry, and then return to California with his bride. Louis Pellier asked his brother to bring back with him cuttings of the choicest fruit trees, which he felt sure would grow well here.

In 1856, Pierre arrived in San Francisco with his wife and a third brother. Part of their luggage included two large trunks filled with twigs which had been stuck into potatoes to keep them moist. In addition, the trunks were packed with sawdust to aid moisture retention. Most of these cuttings were from the famous Prune d'Agen, widely accepted in France as the finest plum for drying.

Louis Pellier set to work grafting these twigs to the native wild plum stocks on his land. Within a few years he had a fine orchard of this new prune-plum, and soon more and more surrounding land was being planted in prune orchards.

In Gilroy, much of the land you will recall was owned by Henry Miller. After Miller's death in 1916, hundreds of acres were put on the market. Many who bought parcels of what was once grazing land, converted their acreage to orchards. From that time through the 1950's, the prune became one of Gilroy's, and indeed one of our county's biggest industries.

Because of the abundance of prunes, and later apricots, in south county, the local farmers formed a Co-Op Dryer about 1920. This system greatly facilitated the dehydration process, in addition to cutting down on each individual farmer's expenses. Most of the dryers are still standing on Leavesley Road, near Monterey Highway. Many of them have been converted to rental storage units in recent years.

Today it is a sad fact that more and more orchards are being uprooted to make room for additional housing developments. The ax has been a little slower to fall in Gilroy where there are still many hundreds of acres of prunes. In late March they provide for us one of the joys of a rural environment, a sea of white, fragrant blossoms which usher in springtime.

In this 1915 photograph, thousands of prunes are being dried in the south county sunshine.

According to the Prune Growers Association, three out of four prunes in the world today still come from California. Although our area is not a prime contributor as it once was,

Prunes were once a major industry in Gilroy. The Sunsweet plant, pictured here, operated until the late 1970's.

hopefully the prune orchards will not vanish entirely from our midst.

Seeds

Even before 1900, Santa Clara County had one of the largest seed farms in the world, C.C. Morse and Company in the Santa Clara area. The climate here is ideal for seed production. The almost uninterrupted sunshine during the summer months permits the seeds to thoroughly ripen for highest yield. At one time over 2,000 acres in the San Jose region were planted in flowers and vegetables for seeds.

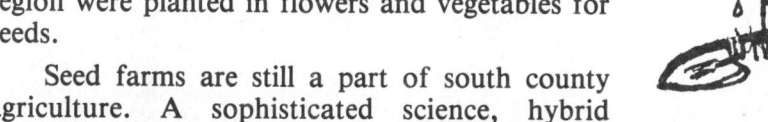

Seed farms are still a part of south county agriculture. A sophisticated science, hybrid research at these seed facilities continues to develop strains, particularly of vegetables, that can at least in part supply the food needs of people around the world. Such research has made significant in-roads toward raising the self-sufficiency level of Third World countries in particular.

From Japan

When the cry of "Gold!" was heard 'round the world, many Japanese heeded that cry, intending to return home eventually with their new-found wealth, and buy farms and businesses there. Very few realized this dream. Still, many Japanese were satisfied to stay here once they discovered the fine agricultural opportunities.

But even this pursuit was to be stifled for many years. The Asiatic Exclusion Act passed by Congress at the turn of the century ruled that these immigrants were not eligible for citizenship. Later this circumstance was further complicated by the Alien Land Law of 1913 which decreed that those ineligible for citizenship could not purchase land. The best they could do was to lease land in three year terms.

Undaunted, the Japanese did just that. One of the first to arrive here was Tamizo Nakashiki who settled south of town in 1902. In 1904, the parents of Shigeru Yamane, who still farms land on Frazier Lake Road, came to Gilroy, having first worked in the pineapple and cane fields of Hawaii.

The Yamanes and the Kishimuras were among the first to grow large quantities of bell peppers in our valley.

These families and others like them tilled the earth, which was by the way, often the less desirable tracts of land. Still these supreme horticulturalists were able to render the ground productive. Nearly all of the strawberries and tomatoes grown here in the early 1900's were produced by the Japanese.

More Japanese settled here following the 1906 earthquake in San Francisco in which many of them lost everything. The Fugimotos were one such family. Once established here, they operated a store at the corner of Seventh and Monterey Streets for some thirty years.

Among the first to raise large amounts of garlic in the Gilroy area was Kiyoshi "Jimmy" Hirasaki. He was sent to the United States in 1914 for schooling, settling first in Milpitas. He was then sixteen years old. Not long after that, he came to Gilroy and learned the seed business under the loving guidance of a Gilroy grower who appreciated the young man's quick mind and ambitious spirit.

After a time, Hirasaki branched out on his own, growing seeds on leased Willson ranchland. He returned to Japan in 1928 and brought his bride back to California. In the years to follow, like many others, the Hirasakis bought land in their children's names, since citizenship was a birthright to their offspring born here. The families would form corporations, usually with Caucasians, and the corporation served as guardian until the "owners" came of age.

Hirasaki had land along Pacheco Pass. By 1941, over 1,500 acres were planted in garlic, making him the largest producer in the state at that time. Hirasaki also raised celery, green peas, broccoli, and other vegetable crops.

A large farmhouse on the property was utilized in part when a picturesque new home was constructed on the site in 1941. Many parts of this dwelling came from the Japanese Pavilion of the 1938-39 World's Fair on Treasure Island. Hirasaki purchased them when the building was dismantled after the fair. This lovely home still stands and is now the residence of Hirasaki's daughter and son-in-law, Mr. and Mrs. Lawson Sakai. The gardens there are a work of art. Mrs. Sakai explained that their creation was the genius of the same landscape architect who designed the Japanese Pavilion garden exhibit at the fair.

As spokesman for the Japanese community here, Hirasaki was one of the first to be picked up by the FBI in the panic that followed the Japanese attack on Pearl Harbor. Sadly, many Gilroy families destroyed all indications of their Japanese heritage during that period--heirlooms, photographs, records and diaries. Hirasaki was found not guilty of disloyalty and was later released.

Following the war years, which the family voluntarily spent in Colorado, the Hirasakis returned to Gilroy. Fortunately, during their absence, their home was not subjected to the vandalism that many other Japanese families encountered upon their return.

In 1948, Jimmy Hirasaki built a shipping warehouse near Tenth and Alexander Streets. From here, fresh valley produce was packed and iced in refrigerator cars, then sent by train to midwestern and east coast markets. One specialty, boxed under the label "Jimmy's Choice", was a hearty celery variety. It's freshness could withstand the cross-country journey, thus it was much in demand and brought a good price.

In the 1950's the old farmhouse mentioned above was moved to land near Tenth and Alexander Streets which Jimmy Hirasaki donated to the Japanese Community League. To this day, the building is the meeting place of the League and is known as the Japanese Community Hall.

Before we conclude this section, I would like to also mention the Nagareda brothers. Earlier in this century they enriched the alkaline soil of the previously unproductive Bolsa area, and brought this acreage into full cultivation. Farming is still the livelihood of some members of the Nagareda family. They are among the many Japanese who have contributed so much to the success of Gilroy's agricultural industry.

Celery is being prepared for shipment at the Hirasaki Farms. This photograph was taken in the early 1950's.

Europeans and the Dairy Industry

Many of the newcomers settling here had their roots in Europe as we've indicated previously. They brought with them the skills and traditions of their native lands. As you are aware, our valley's floor is laced with several streams or creeks, the Llagas, the Uvas, the San Felipe to name a few. The succulent grasses that grow along these streams are advantageous for dairying. Early dairyman Richard Brem also noted that the absence of heavy alkali in our water was another secret of our fine dairy products. The milk must be heated to 160 degrees for processing where alkali is present. Brem stated that this excessive heat forces the butterfat out of the milk. His milk was never heated above 102 degrees, he claimed.

Several dairies began between the years of 1855-60. The largest in this area and in the state was owned by Oscar and Henry Reeve, brothers who

Built in 1908, this creamery made fine butter for many years.
The historic building still stands on Martin Street.

had over eight hundred cows. They sold both milk and cheese locally, and once a week large orders of cheese were hauled to Alviso for shipment to other areas of the state.

Among the others who established cheese producing dairies were: Rodney Eschenberg, Albert Dexter, S.M. Maze, Samuel Rea, E.A. Sawyer, August Gubser, Jacob Hosang, Tracy Learnard, Alex Watson, and J.H. Ellis. By 1896 over one million pounds of cheese per year were being produced in Gilroy. The prices usually ranged between 6^c and 10^c per pound!

Tracy Learnard was one enterprising young dairyman who urged his fellow farmers to form a co-op so that machinery and labor expenses could be shared. Lacking group support initially, he went ahead anyway, and founded a creamery on the family ranch which was about 3½ miles west of town. It wasn't long before his neighbors responded. Products issuing from this creamery bore the Live Oak label.

In 1908, with some financial assistance from his father, Learnard expanded his operation and also moved it to a more central location. The Live Oak Creamery at the corner of Martin and Railroad Streets opened for business in April of that year. Mr. Learnard's machinery there could at first turn out six hundred to seven hundred pounds of butter each day. Later he increased production to one thousand pounds per day. This was a real boom to the local dairymen.

The Live Oak Creamery building is still standing. It has been nominated for The National Register of Historic Places. The present owners have plans to restore the building which has in recent years been empty and subject to vandalism.

Dairying continued to be a major industry in Gilroy well into this century. Lester & Fravi, Silacci & Silva, Frasetti, Bettencourt & Sperber are among some of the families who made Gilroy "The Dairy Capital of California" from 1910 to about 1940. The industry has been drastically reduced in the ensuing decades, but it is not entirely gone. A handful of families are keeping alive one of Gilroy's earliest and most successful enterprises.

The Gilroy Brewery..........Gilroy's Tobacco Industry

Henry Miller was not the only German immigrant to leave his mark on Gilroy's history.

When he came to America from Germany, Adam Riehl first settled in Missouri. He headed west in 1853, and after a stint at the mines, lived for awhile in San Francisco.

In 1867 he moved to Gilroy. The following year he built the Gilroy Brewery along Monterey Street between Sixth and Seventh Streets. He apparently had a partner in the firm, Jacob Reither, or at least received financial backing from him. Reither, also a native of Germany had established himself in Gilroy in the mid-1850's.

The Brewery was a favorite meeting place for many of the menfolk of Gilroy for many decades. It's doors were closed in 1919.

The Brewery was a success, and Riehl ran it until 1877 when he sold to Adam Herold. Herold made improvements to the building and increased production. In 1884 Michael Casey bought into the brewery. Two years later, when Herold decided to pursue a political career, Casey bought him out.

Under Casey's management the Gilroy Brewery did a thriving business, and remained an important fixture in the community until Casey retired in 1919 and terminated the business.

It should be noted that all of the men connected with the Brewery's management were upstanding community leaders. Adam Riehl served as mayor from 1878-80; Jacob Reither held said office between 1882-86; and Michael Casey was also a Gilroy mayor in the years 1894-98. All three men served on our common council. In addition, Riehl served a term in California's State Assembly and Adam Herold was State Treasurer for a time.

In spite of the respectability of the business, its existence in town did not please everyone. Some saw it as "the root of all evil". Perhaps the rumblings of Prohibition were a part of Michael Casey's decision to shut-down his operation. It is doubtful that the occasional flare-ups of local dissension played any part. As to the brewing secrets which created the choice lager and steam beer of Gilroy, they disappeared when Michael Casey closed the doors of the Gilroy Brewery.

* * * * *

Another important crop/industry for a time in Gilroy's earlier days was tobacco. The bulk of this product was raised in the San Felipe area. J.D. Culp built a cigar factory two miles west of town in 1862, the location of which changed several times in the years to follow. Gilroy's tobacco exhibit won a silver medal, pictured here, at the Panama-Pacific International Exposition in San Franciso in 1915.

Tobacco Exhibit Award, 1915

Southern Europeans...Wineries and the Canning Industry

Over the years people from the sunny countries around the Mediterranean Sea also found their way to our valley. Open land was scarce in their homelands, and many of the immigrants who arrived here came with little else but their dreams of farming a piece of ground they could call their own.

Finding a similar climate in Gilroy to that of their native land, many of the Italians settling here planted vineyards, orchards, and fields of vegetables, the same things they'd farmed back home.

Giacomo Princevalle arrived in California in the gold rush years, but it wasn't until the late 1860's that he settled in Gilroy. He opened a fruit stand which grew to be a fully-stocked grocery store. In 1904, his son James took over the business, and later also had an ice cream parlor and a candy shop in town. James Princevalle served on our city council and was mayor from 1920-32.

The Angelo Sturla family first lived in San Franciso when they arrived in the United States in 1862. Once becoming Gilroy residents, they raised fresh vegetables for market in the Old Gilroy section of town. There are many generations of Sturlas still residing in our community.

Charles Porcella is another name you'll recognize. A native of Genoa, he first worked for Miller & Lux upon settling here. In 1888, he established the store on Monterey Steet which is still operated by his son George.

Eduardo Scagliotti found his way here in 1900. Like Mr. Porcella, he too was employed by the vast Miller & Lux enterprise. Several years later, he and three of his brothers leased a 200 acre ranch on Watsonville Road. Here they raised prunes, apricots, apples and grapes. By 1912, Eduardo had secured a bonded winery license and had begun making wine for commercial use.

A typical scene early in this century. Many families settling in the Gilroy area planted orchards.

In 1915, the brothers purchased their own one hundred twenty acre tract, and in this same year, Eduardo resigned from Miller & Lux. Five years later, Eduardo bought out his brothers. He was successful on his own, raising mostly grapes.

As John Roffinella, long-time grape broker explained, during the Prohibition years, families with many acres in vineyards did well. Tons of grapes were shipped to the east coast and other areas because home wine-making was not illegal. Grapes were in demand and could command a high price. Grapes were sold to local families as well, by growers such as Eduardo Scagliotti. He and other local vintners also made sacramental wine, which was within the law.

Eduardo's son Peter took over the family's opertion, Live Oaks Winery, in the late 1930's. Located along the Hecker Pass Highway, it is one of the numerous family wineries to the west of Gilroy. This area is often referred to as "little Italy". Fortino, Hecker Pass, also in the Fortino family, Conrotto, and Giretti--all of these families have carried on a proud tradition. Bertero

Winery, founded in 1917 by Alfonso Bertero, was sold in 1980 to Summerhill Vineyards of Carmel, and now goes by that name.

The Kirigin Cellars should be mentioned here too. Located deep in the Uvas (Spanish for grapes) Valley along Watsonville Road, it was first the winery of Pietro Bonesio. Bonesio founded his operation in 1915 in the Rucker district, and then moved to this site in 1921. His sons, Victor and Louis took over the bulk of the business in 1932. Their quality wines were bottled under the Uvas label.

The winery grounds were originally a part of the Solis Rancho. The home on the property dates back to approximately 1830, and is one of the oldest structures in the county. It is listed in the Santa Clara County Heritage Resource Inventory.

Vineyards have thrived in our valley for over a century. Gilroy's family wineries are popular with the local people and the tourists.

Nikola Kirigin Chargin and his family bought the winery from the Bonesios in August of 1976. The Chargins are from Croatia originally. They produce a variety of fine wines, and offer gracious, old-world hospitality at their facility as do the owners at all of Gilroy's fine wineries . . . those mentioned and Rapazzini's, Thomas Kruse, Sarah's Vineyard, and the San Martin Tasting Cellars to the north and south of Gilroy as well. All are to varying degrees involved in community projects, which seek to promote not only the wine industry, but the Gilroy area as well.

In his book "The Wines of America", Leon D. Adams pays our wineries, among others in the county, quite a compliment when he states, "In fact the visitor who travels south instead of north from San Francisco may get a clearer concept of the past, present and future of premium California wines."

* * * * *

We spoke earlier of the increased cultivation of row vegetable crops. Production became such that not everything grown here could be sold fresh. The logical solution . . . ? In 1907 the Bisceglia brothers Joseph, Bruno and Alfonso, established a cannery on Lewis Street. For a time one of their foremen was young Gennaro Filice who came to Gilroy from Cosenza, Italy, at the age of sixteen.

Later Mr. Filice headed a group of his relatives who founded another cannery with the Perelli brothers. Theirs was the well-known

F & P label. In 1913 the Bisceglia brothers sold out to Filice and Perelli.

About 1960, F & P became a part of the large California Canners and Growers Association. This large canning plant, still on Lewis Street continues to be an important industry for Gilroy.

* * * * *

I'd like to insert here that descendents of the many families, particularly from Italy and Portugal, who played a part in Gilroy's development continue to observe the traditions of their homelands. The Italian Catholic Federation, Gilroy Branch No. 28, was inaugurated in May of 1931. Through the years they have carried on social and service projects, extending a hand of fellowship into the community.

Likewise is the spirit of the Portuguese. Every spring they celebrate the Festival of the Holy Ghost, which reenacts an old Portuguese legend. A festive parade with queens and sidemaidens in beautiful costumes, as well as many marching units, is held along Eigleberry Street. A special Mass and a dinner dance at the IFDES Hall are all a part of this annual tradition.

The salad bowl analogy comes to mind again; our ethnic groups maintain their individuality, while contributing to the rich cultural whole that is Gilroy.

The Garlic Capital

We shouldn't leave our discussion of agriculture without saying a little more about our renowned garlic.

We noted that garlic has been grown here since the early 1900's. As the decades progressed, more and more acreage was cultivated in garlic, largely

Garlic growing in nearby fields is a familiar sight in Gilroy.

because our climate is most advantageous to the best production of this plant.

For some time Joseph Gubser Jr. has been called "The King of Garlic". His grandfather, August Gubser, came to California from Switzerland in the late 1880's. After a time in Tres Pinos, he settled here, in the Frazier Lake area, as a dairyman. Joseph Gubser Sr., one of five children born to August and Carrie Gubser, grew garlic in our valley for nearly fifty years. Joseph Jr. is following in his father's footsteps, and also operates a large garlic processing business along Monterey Highway, just south of town.

Statistics vary from year to year, but over 100 million pounds of garlic are produced in our area each year. About one quarter of that amount is sold fresh. The bulk is dehydrated and then converted into a variety of food products . . . flakes, powders, salts and the like. The garlic industry is a large employer in Gilroy, from field work, to the processing plants, to marketing and sales. Gilroy Foods and Foremost Gentry, both located along the Pacheco Pass Highway are prime examples. From our home base, garlic products are sold worldwide.

In 1979, growing out of an idea of Dr. Rudy Melone, president of our Gavilan College, and a few of his ambitious cohorts, our Garlic Festival came into being. Beginning with a garlic-laced Rotary luncheon, a few months later the entire community was invited to a garlic gala held at the A & D Christopher Ranch. Among other crops, the Christophers raise a large amount of garlic. This community-minded couple continue to play an active part in the Festival each year.

Val Filice, another garlic farmer, has also been a part of the core team from the start, heading up the fine food forces at the featured attraction of the fair, "Gourmet Alley".

In addition to the dedicated round-the-year planning of the Festival Committee, hundreds of volunteers give hundreds of hours to make the Garlic Festival the success that it is. It is a wonderful "happening" which generates a great deal of positive energy in our community.

Gilroy now has a sister city, thanks to garlic. Monticelli D'Ongina, located in northern Italy, is striving to become the "Garlic Capital of

Courtesy of Dr. Melone

Dr. Rudy Melone, right, presents the sister cities charter to the mayor of Monticelli D'Ongina.

Italy". City officials there read a wire service article about Gilroy and its festival some time ago. They wrote to our local government, suggesting the sister cities plan. Dr. Melone and his wife were planning a trip to Italy in the summer of 1981, and added this community to their itinerary. They presented a formal charter and our good wishes to the people of Monticelli D'Ongina. A cultural exchange program is underway, and the hospitality is warm on both sides of the Atlantic!

The Grange

The Grange, a national fraternal association of farmers founded in 1867, has been a part of Gilroy's history as well. Our local chapter, No. 398, was organized in December of 1922 with F.E. Stelling serving as the first Master. They met for nearly twenty years in the old Masonic Hall on Monterey Street. In the early 1940's, the Gilroy Grange purchased a building on Swanston Lane which had been a Japanese school. This has been the Grange Hall since then.

The Grange is a fellowship of over ½ million people with local, district, state and national governing levels. The Grange seeks to promote the virtues of home, family, community involvement and agriculture. A self-help organization, members work closely with their local governments to improve the quality of life in their communities. In Gilroy, the Grange was very instrumental in establishing our rural mail delivery system and our Rural Fire Department. Look for their fine exhibits when you attend the County Fair.

The Chinese

You may find it interesting to know that at one time a part of Gilroy was known as Chinatown.

Many Chinese men first ventured overseas to the United States in the 1860's, hiring into the labor force involved in building the Transcontinental Railroad. When the rail line was completed, many of these workers only stayed in California long enough to secure space on board a ship heading for their homeland. Some, however, decided to settle here.

By the early 1900's, Gilroy had a Chinese population of approximately two hundred people, some working out on ranches and the rest living in town. Chinatown was the section of Monterey Street between Seventh and Eighth Streets. Shops along this stretch included a general store, operated by Low Dan, a restaurant called Kwong Chow Low, two coffee shops, the Young Fu Wu and the Ming Wong, a laundry, a Chinese drug and herb store known as Quen Wo, and several gambling halls. There was a large grocery store where Baja Burgers is today.

Some of the Chinese raised vegetables on leased land along the east side of Monterey Street. When ripe, they'd harvest enough at one time to fill their bamboo baskets which were suspended from either end of a pole and were carried on the back, balanced on their shoulders. These farmers made a modest living selling their crops from door to door in the neighborhoods close to Chinatown.

There were few women in Chinatown, because most of the men could not afford to bring a wife from China. Those who were here observed the dress code of their homeland, as did the men. The photograph here shows the pajama-type of loose-fitting pants and tunic top which were the standard costume for everyday use by both men and women. For festive occasions the ladies enjoyed dressing up in high-collared gowns of lovely bright silken material.

A Chinese CKS Temple was a central part of Chinatown life. It was located on the alley in back of our present-day Garcia's restaurant and was called Joss House. In the backroom of this facility, aged, ill, and destitute men were housed. This was the site of much sorrow. Here many people lived out their final days, frequently smoking opium to ease their despair.

Chinese New Year was the most important annual festival. Red was the featured color, because it represented life and good fortune. Red tablecloths were used on family tables and red envelopes containing money were handed out for good luck. The Chinese made good on all their debts at year's end, if at all possible. The New Year, they believed, should be started clear and obligation free.

*Courtesy
Ralph Rambo*

A large banquet was held each year, and the city's dignitaries were invited. Strings of firecrackers were set off at evening's end to chase away any bad spirits.

Unfortunately, Chinatown was the scene of violence on more than one occasion. Groups called Tongs were formed in many communities to provide mutual protection, assist the poor and arrange medical treatment for those in need. However, some Tongs became gangs employing mob-like tactics. Protection became something that shopkeepers were expected to pay for. When extortion demands weren't met, gunmen raided the businesses. Several murders occurred this way in Gilroy's Chinatown. On one occasion, in the 1920's, in addition to the gunfire there, the thugs set fire to Low Dan's general store. A major portion of Chinatown burned to the ground in that blaze. Many of the residents were forced to go elsewhere, to Chinese neighborhoods in San Jose or San Francisco, until their businesses could be rebuilt. Many never returned.

In the 1930's Chinatown experienced a temporary resurgence. The gambling halls and game rooms were popular with many. People motored in from out of town for an evening of fan tan, black jack, or keno. There were even slot machines in these establishments, as the gambling laws were not strictly enforced. The Chinese restaurants were an attraction as well.

With the war years of the early 1940's, the families began moving out of Chinatown. Many of them resettled in the San Francisco area. Eventually the Chinatown section was no more.

But again, Gilroy's rich cultural tapestry is in part woven by the many Chinese-Americans who continue to make our city their home. The Chinese New Year Festival is a part of their tradition that is with us still . . . Gung Hay Fat Choy!

The Newspapers of Gilroy

We need to backtrack in time once again to review the establishment and growth of our local newspaper.

Our earliest newspaper was the *Gilroy Advocate*, started by G.M. Hanson and C.F. Macy. The first edition was published on September 12, 1868. In its fledgling days, the *Advocate* office was located in the second story of a building at the corner of Monterey and Sixth Streets, present-day site of Hall's of Gilroy Clothing Store. The paper was published every Saturday. Apparently Hanson's son took over for Macy after only a few weeks of operation. The paper was published for nine years with a succession of various publishers.

In the early days the staff was quite small. Often there was just the editor/publisher, the print man, and usually only one reporter to gather the stories.

GILROY ADVOCATE

GILROY, SANTA CLARA CO., CALIFORNIA. SATURDAY, MARCH 23, 1918   WHOLE NUMBER 2408

The Gazette has the largest Circulation, Prints the most News, Produces the best Results to Advertisers

GILROY, SANTA CLARA COUNTY, CALIFORNIA, FRIDAY, MAY 17, 1907.   NO. 3

Established 1868

Advocate, Vol. 99, No. 158
Dispatch, Vol. 40, No. 157   11   GILROY, CALIFORNIA, 95020 — Friday, April 1, 1966   Ninety-Ninth Year, No. 157

The *Advocate* really came to fruition in 1877 when F.W. Blake took over as publisher. He remained at the helm until his death in 1907. Under Blake's direction, the paper continued detailed accounts of local events, but was also infused with a generous coverage of national and world news.

Even before the turn of the century, there were numerous other small newspapers in Gilroy. The *Gilroy Union*, the *Gilroy Telegram*, and the *Gilroy Independent* were among those early attempts, but few of them endured for long. By the middle 1880's only the *Gilroy Gazette* became a strong competitor of the *Advocate*.

In 1929 the *Gazette* became a part of the *Gilroy Dispatch* which had begun publication in 1925. The *Dispatch*, under the direction of John N. Hall and Thomas Losey roared in like a lion, with issues appearing six days of the week. Gilroy was one of the smallest towns in California in those days to have a daily paper. The *Advocate* and *Gazette* were only weeklies. Hall's interest was bought out within a year by Hoyd E. Smith, who was from the Red Bluff area.

During the Depression years, the *Advocate* could no longer financially function as an independent. Will Blake, who had taken over after his father's death, remained with the paper until a short time before it was sold to Smith in 1934, and absorbed by *The Dispatch* the following year.

In the late 1970's *The Dispatch* was purchased by the McClatchy chain which headquarters in Sacramento. The paper continues to be managed, however, by a local staff. *The Dispatch* focuses on South County news, but is continually expanding its capabilities.

The fine new facility on south Monterey Street opened in the summer of 1981, and in November of that year, the paper moved to daily (Mon-Fri) publication. The format was greatly expanded at this time with the newspaper's addition of a sophisticated wire service satellite system beamed from New York.

Even with the increased national and global coverage, *The Dispatch* continues to offer the community a newspaper whose core is the issues, news, and human interest stories of the people it serves.

Healthcare for Gilroy

The first hospital in Gilroy was called The Gilroy Private Hospital. It was located on the second floor of a building at the corner of Monterey and Fifth Streets where The Card Carousel is today. Dr. Jonas Clark established this approximately twelve-bed facility in 1899. He was a distinguished physician, serving as Superintendent of the Santa Clara County Hospital from 1910-13. Later he also served for ten years as the District Surgeon for the Southern Pacific Railroad. He was at one time President of the Santa Clara County Medical Society as well.

Dr. James Thayer and Dr. Jonas Clark in 1890, standing in front of their offices.

His son John also became a physician who practiced in Gilroy well into this century. His daughter Marie was the head nurse of our school district for about thirty years.

Dr. James Thayer pictured here with Dr. Jonas Clark was another highly-regarded local practitioner. The family home that he had built in the 1890's on the corner of Martin and Railroad Streets is still standing, a handsome Victorian-style dwelling, and also listed in the Santa Clara County Heritage Resource Inventory. Dr. Thayer served a term as District Surgeon for the Southern Pacific Railroad in addition to his private practice.

In the late 1920's Linwood W. Wheeler gave three and one-half acres of land to the City of Gilroy on which to build a hospital. The result was our (Old) Wheeler Hospital building located on Fifth Street between Carmel and Princevalle Streets. Built in 1929 in the Mediterranean style, it was a thirty-five bed facility, and served the community until our newer hospital was constructed in 1962. Today's Wheeler Hospital sits nearly back to back with the

A gift from Linwood W. Wheeler made possible this first major hospital in Gilroy, built in 1929.
Courtesy Robin McGinnis

original structure, and faces Sixth Street. Old Wheeler is still used for hospital work. The Red Cross is located in the front entrance room. Some business offices, including public relations, data processing, purchasing and computer accounting are still housed in this building as well. The sewing circle of the Wheeler Hospital Auxiliary also meets here each week, and has done so since 1929.

Wheeler Hospital continues to expand and improve, as it faces the challenge of serving a growing community.

Built in 1962, our current hospital facility continues to grow with the community.

Some of Those Who Gave Generously to Gilroy

Linwood Wheeler

More needs to be said about Linwood W. Wheeler. He was a philanthropist in every sense of the word. He came to Gilroy in 1910. He was born in New York, but spent most of his growing years in Wisconsin. He took his

Chamber of Commerce members stringing redwood garlands to decorate Monterey Street for the holidays in 1929 include: left to right, Irvin Hollister, Bill Blaettler, Dr. John Clark, Mayor James Princevalle, Unknown, and Linwood Wheeler.

turn at prospecting, worked on the railroad, and then eventually went into the seed business. He and a partner took control of Pieters-Wheeler Seed Company, and in time Wheeler took over sole ownership.

Mr. Wheeler gave generously to Gilroy. He offered the funds to build the following: the old Elks Lodge Building on Monterey Street, the initial Wheeler Hospital, the Wheeler Auditorium on Sixth Street, and he also donated the land which was for years the Gymkhana grounds. Mr. Wheeler was a supporting friend to many small businesses in town, particularly in the crucial early Depression years when many local merchants were hard-pressed to remain solvent.

The city mourned the loss of this fine man and his lovely wife when they were both killed in a tragic automobile accident in June of 1944.

Caroline Amelia Hoxett

We should also review in more depth the contributions to our city from a fine lady, Caroline Amelia Hoxett. The Hoxetts came to Gilroy from

Massachusetts in 1868. Mr. Hoxett started one of the first bakeries in town.

The couple built an attractive home on Fifth Street in 1868-69 which continues as a private residence today.

Mrs. Hoxett, a woman of means in her own right, bought the old tennis court at the corner of Fifth and Church Streets in the early 1900's. She then gave the land to the city as the site for the Carnegie Library which was built in 1910, and is now our Museum. Caroline Hoxett also provided the land for the I.O.O.F. Children's Home. In addition, she was instrumental in securing the town clock for our old City Hall, which you will hear more about later on. She continued to play an active part in our community until her death in 1927.

Caroline A. Hoxett was often called "Gilroy's Benefactress".

More About Some Historic Public Buildings

Numerous times I have mentioned the Carnegie Library/Gilroy Museum. I would like to elaborate on it at this point.

The Gilroy Museum was formally established in 1963, although it had its beginning some three years prior to that date. It was at first housed in the basement area of the then Public Library. This downstairs section had not been finished off when the building was erected in 1910.

The Gilroy Museum on the corner of Fifth and Church Streets was built as a Carnegie Library in 1910.

Courtesy Robin McGinnis

In the late 1950's, the Library and Culture Commission members decided it would be worthwhile to put in permanent flooring and other improvements so that it could be used as a community room. With city council approval, this remodeling was done. Thereafter, the room was the site of various school exhibits, a Music Appreciation Night, a Science Fair, and so forth.

At the suggestion of Armand White, a Commission member, a Pioneer Days exhibit was created in 1960, involving many of the families whose descendents had settled here in the nineteenth century. This exhibit was such a success that the determination was made that Gilroy was ready for a formal museum. Armand White set about immediately, cataloging many donated items, and arranging show cases for their display in this community room. It was all a labor of love for Mr. White. It was largely due to his efforts that we have our fine museum today.

The upper level of the Carnegie building served as Gilroy's library until February of 1975 when the library moved to its present location on Rosanna Street. Renovation of the former library site to accommodate Museum usage was a CETA project, and was completed in less than a year.

Our current Public Library on Rosanna Street opened its doors in 1975.

A dedication ceremony honoring the opening of the upper level was held on January 11, 1976. Mary Prien (Mrs. Roland H.) has been the Director and gracious hostess of the expanded facility since its opening. She worked with Mr. White in the Museum's earliest years, when visiting hours were only for a few hours each week.

* * * * *

Gilroy's first City Hall on the northeast corner of Sixth and Monterey Streets was built in 1905-06. There was a city-wide celebration for the official laying of the cornerstone in November 1905. A zinc box was lowered into place at that time, which contained the traditional newspapers, names of local civic leaders, coins, and so on.

As much as possible, the structure was built by local workers, utilizing local materials. We spoke earlier of the exterior stone, which was quarried at Henry Miller's Glen Ranch property. The architectural firm of Wolfe and McKenzie of San Jose drew up the plans for the building. The actual construction work was under the direction of foreman George Seay.

When completed, the first floor was for use by the Fire Department. The ceilings were high to accommodate the equipment, and the south wall had three large side doors. There was a fifty foot plot behind the building where the animals were sheltered in those days of horse-powered machinery. This back area also contained a courtyard with a fountain and lawns where citizens could enjoy the sunshine.

The second floor housed the first city library, the courtroom and judge's chambers, and there was also a huge meeting room which could hold up to 300 people. Another smaller room was used by the Board of Trade for a kind of Visitor's Bureau, with exhibits which featured local industries and products.

Henry Miller gave $100 to initiate a fund for the town clock. Mayor Dunlap (1904-1908) donated $50, and L.A. Whitehurst also gave $50. For some reason, the contributions were not forthcoming after this. Finally in 1914, Caroline Hoxett, wishing to remain anonymous, donated the $700 balance needed for the purchase and installation of the clock which is still marking time for the citizens of Gilroy. Someone told on her!

Courtesy Robin McGinnis

The Fire Department relocated in 1916, but the police department headquartered at old City Hall from its inception, remained there until 1965 when it was moved to Rosanna Street.

When all the city offices moved into larger quarters in Wheeler Auditorium in the late 1960's, old City Hall was nearly obliterated, and the land used for a parking lot! Through the persistence and tireless efforts of the Gilroy Historical Society, under the direction of Carl Bolfing, this fine structure was preserved for posterity. The building is now leased to the firm of Hoffman & Associates, and plans are underway for its conversion to a restaurant.

The Chamber of Commerce

Just months before the ground was broken for our first City Hall, a group of citizens, many of them local businessmen, held a town meeting in the Viligant Engine Room. The date of this meeting was April 12, 1905. The decision was made at this gathering to organize a society of community groups to promote the general interests of Gilroy and its surrounding area.

This was the beginning of the Gilroy Promotion Society. In 1912, the Society was replaced by the Gilroy Chamber of Commerce. Its purpose, stated at its founding and still applicable today, is as follows: "To advance the commercial, industrial, civic and general interests of the City of Gilroy and its trade area."

Other Names Gilroyans Remember

There are so many individuals and families whose lives were and are interwoven with the development of our city. I wish it were possible to name them all. We will mention at this point a few more which you may recognize.

John E. White was Constable of Gilroy Township for over thirty years. He died in 1934, while serving his ninth term, and is believed to be the longest continuously elected official in Santa Clara County's history. Serving in the days before a large police force and Sheriff's Department existed here, Constable White is fondly remembered for his fairness and even-tempered manner of "keeping the peace". Through the years he worked closely with the City Marshall, always willing to lend a hand when needed. He was the grandfather of my friend George Willson White who has given me such valuable assistance with my research for this story of Gilroy.

While we are speaking of peace officers, I would like to add that today's large force is to be commended for the job they are doing in our community. Working with the schools, churches, emergency shelters, and other civic groups, our Police Department members surely do their best to enhance the quality of life in our city.

Born in Scotland, Alexander Milne became a prominent vintner in the Burchell Road area. He purchased his 380 acre farm in 1881. A learned man, he enjoyed doing experimental plant research on his land, and was regarded as an expert in many agricultural matters. The beautiful pump organ in our Museum was a gift from the Milne family, many of whom still make Gilroy their home.

George Milias Sr. was a native of Yugoslavia and came to San Jose in 1881. He operated a restaurant there for ten years, before settling in Gilroy. In 1897 he was wed to Minnie White. Mr. Milias had fine business sense. He established Milias Hotel, at the southeast corner of Sixth and Monterey Streets in 1922. The architect was the noted William Weeks.

The Milias had a fine restaurant on the ground floor. Another feature was the roof garden area atop the hotel which had more than one room that could be rented for banquets and parties. The hotel had a real exclusive for those days in Gilroy . . . an elevator! The Milias was a favorite with folks travelling north and south along the old 101 Highway. A part of the Milias building is still home to a popular eating place, the Harvest Time Restaurant.

The Milias Hotel on Monterey Street was completed in 1922. It was a favorite spot for travellers. The restaurant had a fine reputation with local folks as well.

While we are in this neighborhood, allow me to insert a few words about the Old Gilroy Hotel, located just a few doors down from the Milias. The business first opened in 1921, as the Louis Hotel and Cafe. In March of 1982, this refurbished facility began life anew. The restaurant and lounge, under Wayne Chirdon's direction, have captured for us in the 80's, the flair and grace of yesteryear. This revitalizing of our downtown area is a healthy trend in our city.

George Milias also acquired extensive acreage in ranchland to the east of town, and had a thriving cattle business.

His son, George Cavanaugh Milias not only ran the hotel for many years, but was also at the helm of the family's cattle business. In addition, he served on our city council and was mayor for two terms, from 1940-54 and from 1956-58. He was also general manager of the Gymkhana Rodeo for a number of years. His daughter and her husband, Carol and Don Silacci, are now in charge of the ranching operation.

George Milias Ranch Brand

George Wallace Milias, son of George C., served our area in the State Assembly. He was Deputy Director of the Fish & Game Commission under the Department of Interior in Washington D.C. at the time of his death in the late 1970's.

The Strand Theatre

There is another Monterey Street building that played a glamorous part in Gilroy's history in the early part of this century.

The Strand looks like any other downtown movie house today. But it was once the most elegant theatre for miles around.

William Radtke was the contractor for The Strand Theatre building which was formally opened December 3, 1921. The builders took pride in the fact that the structure was modern in every way.

The audience area was filled with nine hundred upholstered opera chairs. A $15,000 pipe organ was secured from Robert Morton of San Francisco. The theatre had a formal orchestra pit. There were four large dressing rooms on the stage level for the star performers. The basement contained additional dressing rooms for other cast members. Harry Bannister, for many years one of Gilroy's leading musicians, was the organist for The Strand.

In addition to live performances, popular feature-length films of the day were shown. Children could attend for one dime, and adults paid twenty cents for admission. As you can see in the photo, the entrance was covered by an elaborate canopy arch.

Beginning in 1929, the Elks Club put on annual Christmas shows at the theatre. Many local residents took part in these talent nights, and whenever possible the Elks signed on guest artists as well to help boost attendance. The Christmas gala was one of the highlights of the holiday social season for a number of years. If you've surmised that Gilroy has always been only an agricultural/ranching center, The Strand was one spot where the city basked in some cosmopolitan glitter!

The upper floor of the theatre building was for the use of the Keith Lodge, Free and Accepted Masons, named for John M. Keith, our first town clerk and one of the petitioners for the incorporation of Gilroy. A big assembly room there was used for large banquets and dances, and could be rented by other groups. The smaller front rooms were outfitted for meeting purposes and as club rooms.

The Mill Road Park

Another entertainment spot of the Roaring Twenties in Gilroy was the Mill Road Park, a dance pavilion located along the Bodfish Mill Road (now Hecker Pass Highway) about three miles west of town. The park was established by Harry P. Learnard, son of Tracy Learnard, the Creamery owner. Old-timers will remember the younger Learnard who also operated Radio Hal's on Monterey Street.

The Mill Road Park was a favorite night spot on the old Bodfish Mill Road. Photo taken about 1929.
Courtesy Harry P. Learnard

Mr. Learnard's broadcasting connections made it possible for him to secure live acts from San Francisco, one of the favorites being "The Three Boys". This trio were KGO regulars in those, the days of live radio shows. Unfortunately Mr. Learnard has no photographs of the actual dance pavilion in his memorabilia collection. This sign at the entrance to the driveway is all that was recorded by his camera.

Groups could rent the Mill Road Park building for large functions. The Italian Catholic Federation, Gilroy Branch No. 28 held many of their special dances here. John Roffinella, an active leader in the ICF for many years, shared some colorful accounts of those festive occasions.

The ceiling area of the pavilion had space to rig bundles of balloons. At a given point during an evening, they were released, and showered down on the dancers. On certain nights there would be a real scramble to secure one, for the dancers were informed that several balloons contained numbers. These numbers entitled the recipients to nice door prizes.

The New Year's Eve dance of 1929-30 was a memorable one. The roof was leaking badly in a seam where an addition had been built onto the main room. Harry Learnard said the ICF could have the hall free of charge for that night if they could fix the roof. Time didn't permit the men to tackle this major repair job before the dance, so they improvised. A big washtub with a hole in the bottom of it was placed underneath the leak. Then a small hole was drilled into the floor as well, and the holes were lined up. This way if it rained, the water would be caught and drained right out of the dance hall.

"Well," I had to know (!) "did it rain that night ?"

John's laughing reply . . . "You bet it did! Like a son of a gun!" And he added, "Nobody minded dancing around the washtub. In fact, the water falling into that basin kept a nice rhythm with the music of the band." A more permanent solution to the leak was found shortly thereafter!

The Mill Road Park was in full swing during Prohibition days. Since it was out of the city limits, the local officials didn't rigidly enforce the law, but were around if things got out of hand. On one occasion, Mr. Roffinella recalled that George Easton brought about a hasty

DANCING
MILL ROAD PARK, GILROY
COMPLIMENTARY PASS

Saturday Night, ..., 193......

Signed, ...

Manager

Present at Box Office Federal Tax, 10% of Admission

Courtesy Harry P. Learnard

"keeping of the peace". Easton, who was our City Marshall at the time, and off-duty on this particular evening, was hired to serve as a security guard. A group from Watsonville showed up to "have it out" with a gang from Hollister. Heated words were being exchanged, and big George moved in, grabbed the two leaders, and knocked their heads together. All the troublemakers were in their cars and gone within minutes!

When Harry Learnard took a job with RCA and moved from Gilroy in the early 1930's, the Mill Road Park was closed shortly afterward. The building was eventually dismantled. A film promoting Gilroy was produced by the Chamber of Commerce about 1928, entitled "Know Your City". In that film, there is a brief glimpse of couples dancing at an animated pace in the Mill Road Park pavilion. The Historical Society has had the film restored. This short segment of film is all that remains of Gilroy's once lively night spot.

The Gymkhana

You've seen this word Gymkhana (pronounced jim-con-na) several times in this last part of our story. If you came to Gilroy after 1956, you may wonder "what's a gymkhana?" The word is an English/East Indian one which means a meeting or meeting place for sports events or contests. In particular, it involves sports on horseback.

Gilroy's Gymkhana was a festive yearly rodeo which began in 1929, co-sponsored by the Gymkhana Association and the Gilroy Chamber of Commerce. It was mentioned earlier that Mr. Linwood Wheeler gave the land for the Gymkhana grounds. The arena and surrounding area were located just a little to the north of the present-day athletic field of South Valley Junior High School.

Portable bleacher seats were rented from the Fiesta Committee in San Jose, and provided 5,000 seats. Cowboys and rodeo animals came from every western state to compete in the many events. The townspeople celebrated for the whole week before this weekend rodeo took place. There were two parades, one Saturday morning and one Sunday morning, which went from Seventh Street all the way up Monterey Street to the rodeo grounds. Businesses were asked to close from noon 'til five on these days, and cars were removed from the parade route by ten a.m., or were supposed to be! You can see in the two photographs that not all citizens complied with the request! Professional decorators ran streamers across Monterey Street at all the main intersections, and the shopkeepers added to the gaiety with thematic window displays and banners. A Gymkhana Princess was chosen each year to reign over the festivities.

A parade float with a western band entertains the townspeople along Monterey Street during Gymkhana weekend in 1929. The Martin Hardware Co. in background is where Dick Bruhn's is located today.

Courtesy Harry P. Learnard

The Gymkhana was held until 1956. Not long after, the grounds were put to industrial use. Since the late 1960's, a private committee, again working in harmony with the Chamber, has put a lot of effort into producing our Gilroy Bonanza Days each June. Although there is no longer a rodeo, the Bonanza Days feature a cowboy theme, and many of the same community participation events. Like the Gymkhana, its main purpose is to bring the people of Gilroy together in an atmosphere of fun and friendship.

The Gymkhana parade featured many riding units. This photo was taken about 1937.

I'd like to close this section with "The Gymkhana Song". It is sung to the tune of "Red River Valley". These lyrics were written years ago by Vivian Head. Many of you may recall singing this in your classrooms. Mrs. Head, as choral director for our district, used to travel to all the schools. Each year this song was sung the week before Gymkhana to get the youngsters in a Rodeo mood!

The Gymkhana Song

(Used with permission of Vivian Head)

There's a town at the end of the valley
Where the sun shines so brightly all day.
And the folks are so friendly and jolly,
That they drive all your troubles away.

Oh each year there they have a Gymkhana,
And the folks come from miles all around
For there's ridin' and ropin' and dancin'
Down in Gilroy, the Gymkhana town.

Just to be once again in that valley,
Where the prunes and the apricots grow,
Where the blue hills are softened by shadows
And the cool ocean breeze lightly blows.

Get your chaps and your saddle and blanket,
For you'll soon be a ridin' along.
When it's Gymkhana time down in Gilroy
That's the place where the cowboy belongs.

Times have changed everywhere, but fortunately much of what existed in Gilroy back then is still with us . . . the friendly people, the ocean breezes and sunshine, and though decreased, the orchards of prunes and apricots. Oh, and let's not forget the cowfolks! With all of its growing and changing, Gilroy remains a city that one is proud to call home.

The End of Our Story

The following lines are the opening verses of a poem written to the honor of Caroline A. Hoxett, Gilroy's benefactress, upon her death in 1927. The poem was published in the *Gilroy Advocate* on June 11th of that year, and was simply signed "A Gilroyan".

"The monuments that honor best the dead
Are those which they themselves while living raised.
In coveting not the gift of future praise,
But brightening the paths that others tread."

We have walked many a pathway of the past with some of the determined pioneers who settled this beautiful valley of ours. As I stated at the onset, we have not learned of them all by any means. But then our story really doesn't have an end. We are all involved in building Gilroy's future, tomorrow's history.

And at anytime that we pause to reflect on our beginnings, may we remember that what has been established and bequeathed to us, is now our responsibility to preserve for the generations to come.

Bibliography

J.P. Munro-Fraser, Historian, *History of Santa Clara County, California*. Alley, Bowen & Co., Publishers, 1881. Pacific Press, Oakland, California.

Marjorie Pierce, *East of the Gabilans*. Valley Publishers, Fresno, California, 1976.

Mildred Hoover, Hero Rensch and Ethel Rensch, *Historic Spots in California*. Stanford University Press, 1948.

Genevra S. Snedden, *Docas, Indian of Santa Clara*. D.C. Heath & Co., Boston, 1958.

Eugene T. Sawyer, *History of Santa Clara County, California With Biographical Sketches*. Historic Record Co., Los Angeles, California, 1922.

Hubert H. Bancroft, *The Works of Hubert H. Bancroft: History of California, Volumes XX, XXII, XXIV*. The History Co., Publishers, San Francisco, California, 1886.

Sunshine, Fruit and Flowers: Santa Clara County, California. A souvenir of the San Jose Mercury, 1896.

The Story of Santa Clara County. Revised by the Santa Clara Unified School District, Board of Eductation, 1979.

Gilroy's First Century of Incorporation, 1870-1970. City of Gilroy and the Gilroy Historical Society. Dispatch Printing, June 1970.

Armand White, *History of Gilroy*. Through the cooperation of the Gilroy Chamber of Commerce, circa 1960

**Sketches of Gilroy*, edited and compiled by James C. Williams. Sketches by Gavilan College students and Mr. Williams. Gilroy Historical Society, July 1980.

*Patricia Snar Simon, *Henry Miller, His Life and Times*, for the Gilroy Historical Society, 1980.

Muriel Nelson Beroza, *Sveadal*. Birchtree Press, Paradise Valley, Arizona. Copyright, 1976.

John and LaRee Caughey, *California Heritage, An Anthology of History and Literature*. The Ward Ritchie Press, Los Angeles, California. Copyright, 1962.

Richard Paul Hinkle, William H. Gibbs, III, *Central Coast Wine Tour*. Vintage Image, St. Helena, California. Copyright 1977.

F. Ralph Rambo, *"Lo, the poor Indian of Santa Clara Valley"*. Rosicrucian Press, Ltd. San Jose, California. Copyright, 1967.

The Gilroy Dispatch, Centennial Edition, January 10, 1969.

The Gilroy Dispatch, Centennial Edition, December 21, 1970.

Nancy McCarthy, "Problems plague City Hall during its colorful history". *The Gilroy Dispatch*, September 8, 1966.

Nancy McCarthy, "Japanese immigrants were the first big garlic growers". *The Gilroy Dispatch*, December 21, 1970.

Muriel Millwood, "Gilroy's Chinatown revisited". *The Gilroy Dispatch*, February 14, 1979.

Walt Glines, "Over the Fence with Peter and Harry Giretti". *The Gilroy Dispatch*, December 1, 1976.

Bibliography (continued)

The Gilroy Dispatch, August 1, 1979. (First Garlic Festival edition)

Patricia Loomis, "Signposts" (column) "Little known of early Gilroy settler". *San Jose Mercury News*, October 1, 1976.

Patricia Loomis, "Signposts" (column) "Hanna family a living part of Gilroy's history". *San Jose Mercury News,* November 11, 1977.

Florence Fava, "The Story of the Ohlone" (Indians), Parts I, II, III. *San Jose Mercury News*, July 23, 1972; July 30, 1972; August 6, 1972.

89 Methodist Years in Gilroy, a history prepared by a committee of church members, October, 1942.

Celery, Hirasaki Farms: A photo-story booklet on this celery business, prepared by Hirasaki Farms, circa 1950.

St. Mary's Church, Gilroy (Centennial Book), Charles E. Pillman, Centennial Book Chairman. Histories: Father John T. Dwyer, Carmen F. Filice. December, 1965.

*The books with an asterisk (*) appearing next to them are available for purchase at our Gilroy Museum. *Pieces of the Past* is also sold at the Museum.